Modern Critical Interpretations

Oscar Wilde's
The Importance of Being Earnest

Modern Critical Interpretations

The Oresteia
Beowulf
The General Prologue to
   The Canterbury Tales
The Pardoner's Tale
The Knight's Tale
The Divine Comedy
Exodus
Genesis
The Gospels
The Iliad
The Book of Job
Volpone
Doctor Faustus
The Revelation of St.
   John the Divine
The Song of Songs
Oedipus Rex
The Aeneid
The Duchess of Malfi
Antony and Cleopatra
As You Like It
Coriolanus
Hamlet
Henry IV, Part I
Henry IV, Part II
Henry V
Julius Caesar
King Lear
Macbeth
Measure for Measure
The Merchant of Venice
A Midsummer Night's
   Dream
Much Ado About
   Nothing
Othello
Richard II
Richard III
The Sonnets
Taming of the Shrew
The Tempest
Twelfth Night
The Winter's Tale
Emma
Mansfield Park
Pride and Prejudice
The Life of Samuel
   Johnson
Moll Flanders
Robinson Crusoe
Tom Jones
The Beggar's Opera
Gray's Elegy
Paradise Lost
The Rape of the Lock
Tristram Shandy
Gulliver's Travels

Evelina
The Marriage of Heaven
   and Hell
Songs of Innocence and
   Experience
Jane Eyre
Wuthering Heights
Don Juan
The Rime of the Ancient
   Mariner
Bleak House
David Copperfield
Hard Times
A Tale of Two Cities
Middlemarch
The Mill on the Floss
Jude the Obscure
The Mayor of
   Casterbridge
The Return of the Native
Tess of the D'Urbervilles
The Odes of Keats
Frankenstein
Vanity Fair
Barchester Towers
The Prelude
The Red Badge of
   Courage
The Scarlet Letter
The Ambassadors
Daisy Miller, The Turn
   of the Screw, and
   Other Tales
The Portrait of a Lady
Billy Budd, Benito Cer-
   eno, Bartleby the Scriv-
   ener, and Other Tales
Moby-Dick
The Tales of Poe
Walden
Adventures of
   Huckleberry Finn
The Life of Frederick
   Douglass
Heart of Darkness
Lord Jim
Nostromo
A Passage to India
Dubliners
A Portrait of the Artist as
   a Young Man
Ulysses
Kim
The Rainbow
Sons and Lovers
Women in Love
1984
Major Barbara

Man and Superman
Pygmalion
St. Joan
The Playboy of the
   Western World
The Importance of Being
   Earnest
Mrs. Dalloway
To the Lighthouse
My Antonia
An American Tragedy
Murder in the Cathedral
The Waste Land
Absalom, Absalom!
Light in August
Sanctuary
The Sound and the Fury
The Great Gatsby
A Farewell to Arms
The Sun Also Rises
Arrowsmith
Lolita
The Iceman Cometh
Long Day's Journey Into
   Night
The Grapes of Wrath
Miss Lonelyhearts
The Glass Menagerie
A Streetcar Named
   Desire
Their Eyes Were
   Watching God
Native Son
Waiting for Godot
Herzog
All My Sons
Death of a Salesman
Gravity's Rainbow
All the King's Men
The Left Hand of
   Darkness
The Brothers Karamazov
Crime and Punishment
Madame Bovary
The Interpretation of
   Dreams
The Castle
The Metamorphosis
The Trial
Man's Fate
The Magic Mountain
Montaigne's Essays
Remembrance of Things
   Past
The Red and the Black
Anna Karenina
War and Peace

These and other titles in preparation

Modern Critical Interpretations

Oscar Wilde's
The Importance of Being Earnest

Edited and with an introduction by

Harold Bloom
Sterling Professor of the Humanities
Yale University

Chelsea House Publishers ◇ *1988*
NEW YORK ◇ NEW HAVEN ◇ PHILADELPHIA

© 1988 by Chelsea House Publishers, a division
of Chelsea House Educational Communications, Inc.,
  95 Madison Avenue, New York, NY 10016
  345 Whitney Avenue, New Haven, CT 06511
  5068B West Chester Pike, Edgemont, PA 19028

Introduction © 1988 by Harold Bloom

Printed and bound in the United States of America

10 9 8 7 6 5 4 3 2 1

∞ The paper used in this publication meets the minimum
requirements of the American National Standard for
Permanence of Paper for Printed Library Materials,
Z39.48-1984.

Library of Congress Cataloging-in-Publication Data
Oscar Wilde's The importance of being earnest.
    (Modern critical interpretations)
    Bibliography: p.
    Includes index.
    Summary: A collection of seven critical essays on Wilde's
comedic play "The Importance of Being Earnest" arranged in
chronological order of publication.
    I. Wilde, Oscar, 1854–1900. Importance of being earnest.
[1. Wilde, Oscar, 1854–1900. Importance of being earnest.
2. English literature—History and criticism] I. Bloom, Harold.
II. Title.   III. Title: Importance of being earnest.   IV. Series.
PR5818.I45075 1988   822'.8   87-13779
ISBN 1-55546-022-4 (alk. paper)

Contents

Editor's Note

This book gathers together the best modern critical interpretations of Oscar Wilde's masterpiece of stage comedy, *The Importance of Being Earnest.* The critical essays arc reprinted here in the chronological order of their original publication. I am grateful to Susan Laity for her erudition and judgment in helping me to edit this volume.

My introduction centers first upon Wilde as critical theorist and then traces Wilde's aesthetic in the play. Ian Gregor begins the chronological sequence of criticism by relating *Earnest* to Wilde's other plays, after which Robert J. Jordan balances the childlike fantasy of innocence against the elements of satire in the comedy.

In David Parker's reading, Wilde's farce balances the metaphysical contraries of being and nothingness, while Rodney Shewan examines the play's four-act version in the context of Wilde's career as a dramatist. Beckett and Ionesco enter Katharine Worth's reading, which centers upon the metaphysics of identity in *Earnest.*

Camille A. Paglia, superb and flamboyant chronicler of sexual personae throughout Western literature, attempts to restore the play's repressed or displaced sexual aspects, brilliantly connecting the thematic slippage to the art of the Wildean epigraph. Another restorer of evaded meaning, Joseph Loewenstein, gives us a subtly modulated account of Wilde's aphoristic moral stance in his best comedy.

Regenia Gagnier reminds us that *The Importance of Being Earnest* is conditioned by its marketplace. To see the play as a commodity is to understand Wilde's consummate art of self-advertisement, here and elsewhere.

In this book's final essay, published here for the first time, Susan Laity illuminates *Earnest* by comparing it to W. S. Gilbert's *Iolanthe,* a parallel vision of "the Soul of Man under Victoria." Gilbert permanently parodied Wilde as the poet Bunthorne in *Patience,* where the Aesthete is pilloried as a sham, but Laity exposes the way in which *Iolanthe* is also an aesthetic critique of Victorian middle-class drama and life. She concludes, though, with Wildean rightness, that *Iolanthe* is paradoxically the less original work, even though it comes first, since it shares attributes with what it satirizes, while *The Importance of Being Earnest* transcends genre and prophetically darts forward into the Absurd.

Introduction

Oscar Wilde first published a book in 1881 and after more than a hundred years literary opinion has converged in the judgment that Wilde, as Borges asserts, was almost always right. This rightness, which transcends wit, is now seen as central to the importance of being Oscar. Daily my mail brings me bad poetry, printed and unprinted, and daily I murmur to myself Wilde's apothegm: "All bad poetry springs from genuine feeling." Arthur Symons, like Wilde a disciple of Walter Pater, reviewed the Paterian *Intentions* of Wilde with this exquisite summary: "He is conscious of the charm of graceful echoes, and is always original in his quotations." Symons understood that Wilde, even as playwright and as storyteller, was essentially a critic, just as Pater's fictions were primarily criticism.

Wilde began as a poet, and alas was and always remained quite a bad poet. An admirer of *The Ballad of Reading Gaol* should read the poem side by side with *The Ancient Mariner,* in order to see precisely its crippling failure to experience an anxiety of influence. Of course, Ruskin and Pater also began as poets, but then wisely gave it up almost immediately, unlike Matthew Arnold who waited a little too long. It is deeply unfortunate that the young Wilde gave the world this poem about Mazzini:

> He is not dead, the immemorial Fates
> Forbid it, and the closing shears refrain,
> Lift up your heads, ye everlasting gates!
> Ye argent clarions sound a loftier strain!
> For the vile thing he hated lurks within
> Its sombre house, alone with God and memories of sin.

This dreadful travesty and amalgam of Shelley, Swinburne, the Bible, Milton, and whatnot, is typical of Wilde's verse, and opened him to many attacks which became particularly nasty in America during his notorious lecture tour of 1882. Thomas Wentworth Higginson, whom we remember as Emily Dickinson's amiable and uncomprehending "Mentor," made a public attack upon Wilde's poetic immorality which expanded into an accusation of cowardice for not taking part in the Irish national struggle: "Is it manhood for her gifted sons to stay at home and help work out the problem; or to cross the Atlantic and pose in ladies' boudoirs or write prurient poems which their hostesses must discreetly ignore?" The force of Higginson's rhetoric evaporates for us when we remember that the burly Wilde was no coward, physical or moral, and also when we remember that Higginson, with his customary blindness, linked Wilde's tour to Whitman's work as a wound-dresser in the Washington, D.C., Civil War hospitals: "I am one of many to whom Whitman's 'Drum-Taps' have always sounded as hollow as the instrument they counterfeit." Why, Higginson demanded, had not Whitman's admirable physique gone into battle with the Union armies? A Civil War hero himself, Higginson would have had no scruples about hurling the middle-aged bard and idler into battle. We can credit W. B. Yeats with more insight into Wilde, let alone into Whitman, than Higginson displayed, since Yeats insisted that Wilde was essentially a man of action displaced into a man of letters. In some curious sense, there is a sickness-unto-action in Wilde's life and work, a masked despair that led him to the borders of that realm of fantasy the Victorians called "nonsense" literature, the cosmos of Edward Lear. Lionel Trilling aptly located Wilde's masterpiece, *The Importance of Being Earnest,* in that world, and it seems to me never far from Wilde's work. The metaphysical despair of ever knowing or speaking truth Wilde probably absorbed from his nearest precursor, Walter Pater, whose "Sebastian Van Storck" in *Imaginary Portraits* is a major depiction of intellectual despair. Wilde, deliberately less subtle than his evasive master, Pater, speaks out directly through his mouthpiece, Algernon, in the original, four-act version of *The Importance of Being Earnest:*

> My experience of life is that whenever one tells a lie one is
> corroborated on every side. When one tells the truth one is left
> in a very lonely and painful position, and no one believes a word
> one says.

Wilde's most profound single work is "The Decay of Lying: An Observation," an essay in what now would be called literary theory, brilliantly cast in dialogue form. Vivian, speaking for Wilde, rejects what passes for lying in mere politicians:

> They never rise beyond the level of misrepresentation, and actually condescend to prove, to discuss, to argue. How different

from the temper of the true liar, with his frank, fearless statements, his superb irresponsibility, his healthy, natural disdain
of proof of any kind! After all, what is a fine lie? Simply that
which is its own evidence. If a man is sufficiently unimaginative
to produce evidence in support of a lie, he might just as well
speak the truth at once.

Lying then is opposed to misrepresentation, because aesthetic lying is
a kind of supermimesis, and is set, not against truth or reality, but against
time, and antithetically against time's slave, nature. As Vivian remarks:
"Nothing is more evident than that Nature Hates Mind. Thinking is the
most unhealthy thing in the world, and people die of it just as they die of
any other disease. Fortunately, in England at any rate, thought is not catch-
ing." Nature's redemption can come only through imitating art. We can
believe that Wilde's deathbed conversion to the Church was simply a reaf-
firmation of his lifelong belief that Christ was an artist, not in Wilde a
frivolous belief but an heretical one, indeed an aesthetic version of Gnos-
ticism. Hence Wilde's preference for the Fourth Gospel, which he shrewdly
regarded as Gnostic:

> While in reading the Gospels—particularly that of St. John him-
> self, or whatever early Gnostic took his name and mantle—I see
> this continual assertion of the imagination as the basis of all
> spiritual and material life, I see also that to Christ imagination
> was simply a form of Love, and that to him Love was Lord in
> the fullest meaning of the phrase.

This is Wilde speaking out of the depths, in *De Profundis,* the epistle
addressed to Lord Alfred Douglas from Reading Gaol. G. Wilson Knight,
startlingly linking Wilde and Christ, hints that the ideology of Wilde's
homosexuality was its dominant element, involving the raising of love to
the high realm of aesthetic contemplation. Without disputing Knight (or
Wilde), one can observe that such an elevation is more like Pater than Plato,
more like the lying against time that is the privileged moment than the
lying against mortality that is the realm of the timeless Ideas. As Pater's
most dangerous disciple, Wilde literalizes Pater's valorization of perception
over nature, of impression over description.

II

Wilde stands between Pater and Yeats, between a doctrine of momentary aesthetic ecstasies, phantasmagoric hard gemlike flames, and a vision

of lyric simplification through aesthetic intensity, what Yeats called the Condition of Fire. Pater, and not Lord Alfred Douglas, was Wilde's disaster, as Yeats knew and intimated. Though his immediate sources were in Ruskin, Swinburne, and the Pre-Raphaelites, Pater's sensibility went back to the Keats of the "Ode on Melancholy." Wilde, High Romantic in every way, nevertheless did not have a Romantic sensibility, which is why his verse, derived from all of the Romantics, is so hopelessly inadequate. As a sensibility, Wilde is a fantastic version of Congreve and Sheridan and Goldsmith; an Anglo-Irish wit wandering in the regions of Lewis Carroll, W. S. Gilbert, and Edward Lear, to repeat Trilling's insight again. Nonsense is the truest rejection of mere nature, and the strongest program for compelling nature to cease imitating itself and to imitate art instead. Wilde's theory of criticism achieves magnificence when it extravagantly leaps over sense into the cognitive phantasmagoria of a true theory of the lie, an escape from time into the fantasy of interpretation:

> I know that you are fond of Japanese things. Now, do you really imagine that the Japanese people, as they are presented to us in art, have any existence? If you do, you have never understood Japanese art at all. The Japanese people are the deliberate self-conscious creation of certain individual artists. If you set a picture by Hokusai, or Hokkei, or any of the great native painters, beside a real Japanese gentleman or lady, you will see that there is not the slightest resemblance between them. The actual people who live in Japan are not unlike the general run of English people; that is to say, they are extremely commonplace, and have nothing curious or extraordinary about them. In fact the whole of Japan is a pure invention. There is no such country, there are no such people. One of our most charming painters went recently to the Land of the Chrysanthemum in the foolish hope of seeing the Japanese. All he saw, all he had the chance of painting, were a few lanterns and some fans.

In fact the whole of Japan is a pure invention. There is no such country, there are no such people. That is certainly one of the grand critical epiphanies, one of those privileged moments that alone make criticism memorable. Japan momentarily becomes one with that far and wide land where the Jumblies live, where the Pobble who has no toes and the Dong with a luminous nose dwell together. It is also the land of Canon Chasuble and Miss Prism and Lady Bracknell, the land of cucumber sandwiches where Wilde deserved and desired to live. Call it, surprisingly enough, what Wilde called it, the land of the highest Criticism:

I would say that the highest Criticism, being the purest form of personal impression, is in its way more creative than creation, as it has least reference to any standard external to itself, and is, in fact, its own reason for existing, and, as the Greeks would put it, in itself, and to itself, an end. Certainly, it is never trammelled by any shackles of verisimilitude. No ignoble considerations of probability, that cowardly concession to the tedious repetitions of domestic or public life, affect it ever. One may appeal from fiction unto fact. But from the soul there is no appeal.

Call this Wilde's credo, or, as Richard Ellmann, his crucial scholar, words it: "The Critic as Artist as Wilde." It leads to an even finer declaration, which catches the whole movement from Ruskin and Pater through Wilde and on to Yeats and Wallace Stevens in their critical essays:

That is what the highest criticism really is, the record of one's own soul. It is more fascinating than history, as it is concerned simply with oneself. It is more delightful than philosophy, as its subject is concrete and not abstract, real and not vague. It is the only civilized form of autobiography, as it deals not with the events, but with the thoughts of one's life; not with life's physical accidents of deed or circumstance, but with the spiritual moods and imaginative passions of the mind.

The only civilized form of autobiography: I know of no better description of authentic criticism. What we want from a critic is not ideology and not method, not philosophy and not history, not theology and not linguistics, not semiotics and not technique, not feminism and not sociology, but precisely the moods and passions of cognition, of imagining, of the life of the spirit. If you want Marx and Hegel, Heidegger and Lacan, and their revisionists, then take them, but if you want literary criticism, then turn to Hazlitt and Ruskin, to Pater and Wilde. Wilde's unique gift is the mode of wit by which he warns us against falling into careless habits of accuracy, and by which he instructs us that the primary aim of the critic is to see the object as in itself it really is not.

III

Why then did Wilde rush to social destruction? On February 14, 1895, *The Importance of Being Earnest* opened in London, only six weeks after the opening of *An Ideal Husband*. Wilde was forty-one, in the full possession of his talents and his health. On February 28, he found the Marquess of Queensberry's card waiting for him at the Albemarle Club, with its illiterate, nasty address, "To Oscar Wilde, posing as a somdomite [sic]," in which the weird touch of "posing" failed to amuse him. His note of that day to his close friend Robert Ross has an uncharacteristic tone of hysteria:

> Bosie's father has left a card at my club with hideous words on it. I don't see anything now but a criminal prosecution. My whole life seems ruined by this man. The tower of ivory is assailed by the foul thing. On the sand is my life spilt. I don't know what to do.

Had he done nothing, he would not have found himself, less than three months later, sentenced to two years' hard labor. Richard Ellmann speaks of Wilde's "usual cycle which ran from scapegrace to scapegoat," and presumably Ellmann's forthcoming biography will explain that compulsion. Whatever its psychopathology, or even its psychopoetics, its most salient quality seems to be a vertigo-inducing speed. Freud presumably would have found in it the economics of moral masochism, the need for punishment. Yeats subtly interpreted it as due to the frustrations of a man who should have spent himself in action, military or political. One remembers Lady Bracknell remarking of Jack's and Algernon's father that, "The General was essentially a man of peace, except in his domestic life," an observation that perhaps precludes any vision of Wilde in battle or in political strife. The economic problem of masochism doubtless had its place within Wilde, but few moralists hated pain more than Wilde, and nothing even in Wilde surpasses the moral beauty of the closing pages of "The Soul of Man under Socialism":

> Pain is not the ultimate mode of perfection. It is merely provisional and a protest. It has reference to wrong, unhealthy, unjust surroundings. When the wrong, and the disease, and the injustice are removed, it will have no further place. It will have done its work. It was a great work, but it is almost over. Its sphere lessens every day.
>
> Nor will man miss it. *For what man has sought for is, indeed, neither pain nor pleasure, but simply Life.* (Wilde's italics)

We remember, reading this, that Wilde was Ruskin's disciple as well as Pater's. Ruskin's credo, as phrased in *Unto This Last,* is the prophetic basis for Wilde's social vision:

There is no wealth but Life—Life, including all its powers of love, of joy, and of admiration. That country is the richest which nourishes the greatest number of noble and happy human beings.

Why then was the author of "The Soul of Man under Socialism" and of *The Importance of Being Earnest* so doom-eager? His best poem was not in verse, but is the extraordinary prose-poem of 1893, "The Disciple":

> When Narcissus died the pool of his pleasure changed from a cup of sweet waters into a cup of salt tears, and the Oreads came weeping through the woodland that they might sing to the pool and give it comfort.
>
> And when they saw that the pool had changed from a cup of sweet waters into a cup of salt tears, they loosened the green tresses of their hair and cried to the pool and said, "We do not wonder that you should mourn in this manner for Narcissus, so beautiful was he."
>
> "But was Narcissus beautiful?" said the pool.
>
> "Who should know better than you?" answered the Oreads. "Us did he ever pass by, but you he sought for, and would lie on your banks and look down at you, and in the mirror of your waters he would mirror his own beauty."
>
> And the pool answered, "But I loved Narcissus because, as he lay on my banks and looked down at me, in the mirror of his eyes I saw ever my own beauty mirrored."

Kierkegaard might have called this "The Case of the Contemporary Disciple Doubled." Narcissus never saw the pool, nor the pool Narcissus, but at least the pool mourns him. Wilde's despair transcended even his humane wit, and could not be healed by the critical spirit or by the marvelous rightness of his perceptions and sensations.

IV

The Importance of Being Earnest, in the longest perspective, is one of the handful or so of masterpieces given us by the Anglo-Irish tradition of stage comedy. Congreve's *Way of the World,* Goldsmith's *She Stoops to Conquer,* Sheridan's *School for Scandal* are joined in later times by Wilde's best play and by Shaw's *Pygmalion,* Synge's *Playboy of the Western World,* and Beckett's *Waiting for Godot.* Wilde's *Earnest* stands apart from this company because of its affinities, already cited from Lionel Trilling, with W. S.

Gilbert's libretti and with the fantastic visions of Lewis Carroll and Edward
Lear. Congreve and Sheridan and Shaw intend their representations to
reflect social realities but Wilde (like Beckett) rejects both nature and society
and will not imitate them. He wishes only to originate or set in motion,
which is the root meaning of "earnest." Wilde, Pater's disciple, followed
his master in playing with the finer edge of words, in restoring their etymological meaning, and he charmingly keeps in mind that the ultimate
meaning of his title therefore is "the importance of being original."

Only Oscar is earnest in that sense in his great comedy, because none
of his characters is in any way at all original. They are splendidly outrageous,
but in traditional modes. The most sublimely outrageous is Lady Bracknell,
consummately played by Dame Edith Evans in the film version, where her
exquisite delivery of: "Rise, sir, from this semirecumbent posture" lingers
always in my memory. The conclusion of her interview with Jack is one
of Wilde's triumphs:

> LADY BRACKNELL: In what locality did this Mr James, or
>   Thomas, Cardew come across this ordinary hand-bag?
> JACK: In the cloak-room at Victoria Station. It was given to
>   him in mistake for his own.
> LADY BRACKNELL: The cloak-room at Victoria Station?
> JACK: Yes. The Brighton line.
> LADY BRACKNELL: The line is immaterial. Mr Worthing, I
>   confess I feel somewhat bewildered by what you have
>   just told me. To be born, or at any rate bred, in a hand-
>   bag, whether it had handles or not, seems to me to
>   display a contempt for the ordinary decencies of family
>   life that reminds one of the worst excesses of the French
>   Revolution. And I presume you know what that
>   unfortunate movement led to? As for the particular
>   locality in which the hand-bag was found, a cloak-room
>   at a railway station might serve to conceal a social
>   indiscretion—has probably, indeed, been used for that
>   purpose before now—but it could hardly be regarded as
>   an assured basis for a recognized position in good society.
> JACK: May I ask you then what you would advise me to do? I
>   need hardly say I would do anything in the world to
>   ensure Gwendolen's happiness.
> LADY BRACKNELL: I would strongly advise you, Mr Worthing,
>   to try and acquire some relations as soon as possible, and

to make a definite effort to produce at any rate one
parent, of either sex, before the season is quite over.

JACK: Well, I don't see how I could possibly manage to do
that. I can produce the hand-bag at any moment. It is in
my dressing-room at home. I really think that should
satisfy you, Lady Bracknell.

LADY BRACKNELL: Me, sir! What has it to do with me? You
can hardly imagine that I and Lord Bracknell would
dream of allowing our only daughter—a girl brought up
with the utmost care—to marry into a cloak-room, and
form an alliance with a parcel. Good morning, Mr
Worthing!

(LADY BRACKNELL *sweeps out in majestic indignation.*)

Lady Bracknell's literary lineage is Shakespearean and Johnsonian. Her
rolling periods are indebted to Sir John Falstaff's marvelous mockeries of
pomposity and to Dr. Samuel Johnson's characteristic mode of discourse.
Like Johnson, Lady Bracknell talks for victory, but her involuntary Fal-
staffian gusto qualifies her never-defeated aura. The joy of Wilde's originality is in her asides: "whether it had handles or not," "of either sex," "a
girl brought up with the utmost care," "the line is immaterial." The accent
there is new.

Richard Ellmann, Wilde's definitive biographer, says of *Earnest* that it
"is all insouciance where *Salome* is all incrimination." Sin and guilt, according to Ellmann, are displaced by *Earnest* into cucumber sandwiches and
harmless Bunburying. Biographical criticism is much more to my taste
than, say, deconstruction is, but here even Ellmann nods, and I strongly
deny any understructure of sin and guilt in *Earnest,* a play whose theology
is Pelagian. Wilde's deathbed conversion was a long way off, and there are
no scapegoats in *Earnest,* not even Lady Bracknell.

Innocence is clearly the spiritual condition of everyone in *Earnest,* and
it is what Blake would have called Organized Innocence. Everyone in the
play tells the truth, whether as an afterthought or through hyperbole, or
else in the majestic outrageousness that touches the Sublime in Lady Bracknell: "I see no reason why our dear Cecily should not be even still more
attractive at the age you mention than she is at present. There will be a
large accumulation of property."

Camille A. Paglia shrewdly interprets the four young lovers in *Earnest*
as being versions of what she calls "the Androgyne of Manners." Pragmatically this allies Paglia with Ellmann, since she joyously uncovers the

erotic of High Decadence in the apparent innocence of Gwendolen and Cecily, particularly in the "sexual solipsism" of their diaries. Paglia's particular triumph comes in her High Decadent interpretation of Lady Bracknell's anxiety as to visible deviation from a train schedule, which she reads as a prophecy of that terrible scene of public humiliation endured by Wilde at Clapham Junction.

I admire Paglia's essay the other side of idolatry, but still vote for a more innocent *Importance of Being Earnest,* one in which the oxymoronic "passionate celibacy" is more a wise joke and less a refined perversion. "Nothing that actually occurs is of the smallest importance" is one of Wilde's aphorisms "for the use of the young." Another, yet more germane, is: "It is only the superficial qualities that last. Man's deeper nature is soon found out."

Joseph Loewenstein, gently giving us Wilde as a Blakean or imaginative moralist, catches the truth of Wilde's subtle exaltation of "moral labour," even as the play makes clear it is antinomian on the question of moral laws. I give the last word to Wilde's other masterpiece, "The Decay of Lying": "The only real people are the people who never existed." I stumble about the world booming out Lady Bracknell's pronunciamentos, sustained by her gorgeous reality that so far exceeds our own.

Comedy and Oscar Wilde

Ian Gregor

Repeated revivals of *The Importance of Being Earnest* suggest that it has generally been found a very amusing and a very satisfying play. Accounts of why it is very amusing and very satisfying are harder to come by. In fact, the play seems to be singularly unilluminated by criticism, a curious state of affairs for a work which has frequently been praised in terms which indicate that it is among the best English dramatic comedies.

In trying to understand the kind of success represented by *The Importance of Being Earnest,* two things become clear. The first is that the play has a very precise place in Wilde's development as a dramatist, and that consequently any description of it involves taking into account the nature of his earlier plays; the second, that such a critical description of Wilde's dramatic progress casts a rather unexpected light on some fairly widely held assumptions about the proper relation of the play world to the moral world, form to content, the author to his creation. For Wilde's development as a dramatist is intimately connected with his ability to translate into fully dramatic terms the importance of not being earnest; and the earlier plays contained a lesson which, when fully absorbed by him, led to his most satisfying play.

I

It is possible to regard Wilde's four principal plays as a series of attempts to resolve a particular clash between manners and morals, between style

From *The Sewanee Review* 74, no. 2 (April–June 1966). © 1966 by the University of the South.

and content, between the author and his characters. The problem which faced him, as a dramatist, was a very specific one—that of finding a world fit for the dandy to live in; fit, in the sense that such a world would help to make clear the meaning of the dandy. Considered in general terms, the role of the dandy is defined largely by his alienation from the social world in which he lives. He is the visible emblem of nonattachment. His best audience is himself; his favourite view, that presented him by his mirror. Like the tramp, who was to succeed him in the mythology of a later drama, the dandy is a displaced person, but, unlike the tramp's, this displacement is voluntary, indeed it is ostentatiously sought. It is not in a pair of worn-out boots, but in a buttonhole, that the dandy proclaims himself.

For the dramatist the accommodation of such a figure presents special problems. In so far as his role is mythic and not individualized he requires for his embodiment a special form of play. Drama usually involves its characters in ethical judgments; the dandy elaborately abjures them. Drama is an exploration of character in action; the dandy is self-conscious static, and the art he requires of the dramatist is precisely that which sees the mind's construction in the face. The dramatic role of the dandy would seem to lead into a world where, of necessity, everything was amoral, inconsequential, and superficial. Was it possible to create such a figure and such a world, and yet produce a play which itself would be none of these things? This, basically, was Wilde's problem. He solved it only once with complete success, in his last play, *The Importance of Being Earnest.* In the varying achievement of the three plays which preceded it, however, we can see what were the conditions for such a "solution," and this enables us to understand more clearly the nature of Wilde's single dramatic masterpiece.

Lady Windermere's Fan (1892), Wilde's first play, illustrates very clearly the difficulties that beset a dramatist whose aesthetic ideology includes a belief that manners take precedence over morals and style over content. In this play there are two characters, Lord Darlington and Mrs. Erlynne, who have important sympathies with the dandy view of life. The play, in common with *A Woman of No Importance* and *An Ideal Husband,* has as a central theme of hazards of precipitate and inflexible moral judgment—in this case a wife judging, or misjudging, the nature of her husband's liaison with another woman—and the way in which that judgment has to be modified. And it is in this modification that the dandy has his special role to play. The critical problem in all the plays arises from the nature of the wisdom the dandy dispenses and the relationship of this wisdom to the dilemmas which constitute the plot of the play.

Lady Windermere's Fan opens with the direct confrontation of the dandy and the moralist, Lord Darlington and Lady Windermere:

> LORD DARLINGTON: I think life too complex a thing to be
> settled by these hard and fast rules.
> LADY WINDERMERE: If we had "these hard and fast rules" we
> should find life much more simple.

This is sufficiently indicative of the kind of opposition involved. But of course it is not his attitudes that distinguish the dandy, it is the way in which those attitudes are validated by his mode of expression.

> LORD DARLINGTON: It's a curious thing, Duchess, about the
> game of marriage—a game, by the way, that is going out
> of fashion—the wives hold all the honours, and
> invariably lose the odd trick.
> DUCHESS OF BERWICK: The odd trick? Is that the husband, Lord
> Darlington?
> LORD DARLINGTON: It would be rather a good name for the
> modern husband.
> DUCHESS OF BERWICK: Dear Lord Darlington, how thoroughly
> depraved you are!
> LADY WINDERMERE: Lord Darlington is trivial.
> LORD DARLINGTON: Ah, don't say that, Lady Windermere.
> LADY WINDERMERE: Why do you *talk* so trivially about life,
> then?
> LORD DARLINGTON: Because I think that life is far too
> important a thing ever to talk seriously about it.

Here we have the usual mutual criticism of dandy and moralist with its accompanying paradoxes about things serious and trivial, but the important thing to note is that Darlington's flippant tone authenticates the seriousness of his remarks. He is doing two "serious" things here—one directed at the Duchess of Berwick and the other at Lady Windermere. The first is simple satire, aimed at the social set. Adopting a tone of raffish insouciance—"the game," "the odd trick," "the modern husband"—Darlington parodies current "advanced" views about marriage, views which the Duchess *really* thinks and acts on. Indulgently, she can assume indignation with the coy: "Dear Lord Darlington, how thoroughly depraved you are!" It is a remark which justifies Darlington's satire without disturbing the blithe tone in which it is expressed. But Darlington is also speaking to Lady Windermere, and he intends these remarks as a warning. "The game," "the modern husband" now have a specific reference—to Windermere himself and his relations with Mrs. Erlynne. Darlington, of course, is serious about this, because he is in love with Lady Windermere. But the dandy has his social sense of what is fitting. Public politeness is an outward sign of inward grace; his language, no less than his buttonhole, must be a testimony.

In this exchange Wilde is able to exhibit perfectly the seriousness of the dandy. But it is a precarious poise; the exigencies of the plot are to drive Darlington into an explicit declaration of love, and immediately he forfeits his right to the paradoxical language of the dandy. The fatal place for the dandy's heart to be is on his sleeve. It is interesting to notice that as Darlington fades in the role of the dandy, Wilde tries to keep his element present in the play through one of his friends, Cecil Graham. But, because Graham is nothing more than a choric voice, his wit remains unassimilated into the action of the play, and so remains a collection of cynical obiter dicta, some Wildean epigrams in search of a character. The transformation of Darlington and the coarsening of the dandy in Graham is caught in this exchange:

> LORD DARLINGTON: This woman has purity and innocence. She
>   has everything we men have lost.
> CECIL GRAHAM: My dear fellow, what on earth should we men
>   do going about with purity and innocence? A carefully
>   thought-out buttonhole is much more effective.

If Lady Windermere disturbs Wilde's presentation of Darlington in his role of dandy, she also exercises a distorting effect on his presentation of Mrs. Erlynne. Admittedly the demands of plot are strong here: Mrs. Erlynne has to be seen as supposed temptress of Windermere, and devoted mother to her unsuspecting daughter. But there is no reason why this should affect her credibility, and it is not on the level of her dramatic role that she seems to make contrary demands on the audience. Rather, it is because Wilde presents her alternately as both "inside" and "outside" the action of the play—a protagonist in a moral plot turning, at times, into a Wildean commentator. Her role in the plot makes us react critically to sentiments which we are meant to approve—approve not because they are Mrs. Erlynne's but because they are Wilde's. This crisscross role is sometimes exemplified within a single speech; here, for example, she is speaking to Windermere and leading into a blackmailing request:

> You have a delightful opportunity now of paying me a com-
> pliment, Windermere. But you are not very clever at paying
> compliments. I am afraid Margaret doesn't encourage you in
> that excellent habit. It's a great mistake on her part. When men
> give up saying what is charming they give up thinking what is

charming. But seriously, what do you say to £2000? £2500, I
think. In modern life margin is everything.

The attitude here to compliments, the notion of "saying" controlling
"thinking," has the full Wildean approval, but juxtaposed to the blackmailing threat it merely becomes cynical. And the same applies to the final
phrase, "In modern life margin is everything," which has the authentic
dandyesque ring, but which, in this context, comes over as ruthlessly casual.
It is involvement in plot that affects, in varying degree, the dandyish roles
allocated initially to Lord Darlington and fitfully to Mrs. Erlynne. For
involvement in plot means involvement in a world of judgments, a world
of character.

This discussion of *Lady Windermere's Fan,* concentrating on the particular problem of accommodating the dandy to the moral world, is necessarily
a partial one, and a fuller account would have to indicate that the play is
une pièce bien faite and has an evenness about it which is lacking in *A Woman
of No Importance* and *An Ideal Husband.* More important for our present
purpose, however, is that in the closing episode at least Wilde succeeds in
obtaining just the right tone for dramatically harmonizing the parts of the
dandy and the moralist. A climax in the plot is reached towards the end of
the last act. Will Mrs. Erlynne explain her behaviour by telling Lady Windermere the truth—that she is her mother? Will she tell Lord Windermere
that his wife was thinking of leaving him? In fact she does neither. The
joint happiness of the Windermeres is secured by a discreet omission in the
one case and a false explanation in the other. Lady Windermere is deeply
grateful, and Lord Windermere modifies his condemnation, "She is better
than one thought her"; and the play ends with them giving their respective
estimates of Mrs. Erlynne to her future husband:

> LORD WINDERMERE: Well, you are certainly marrying a very
>   clever woman.
> LADY WINDERMERE (*taking her husband's hand*): Ah, you're
>   marrying a very good woman.

Wilde directs his irony perfectly. Lady Windermere is now very happy,
when her honour is threatened, to see goodness in a well-intentioned lie;
her "hard and fast rules" have been quietly waved aside. Beyond this gently
satiric touch, however, the lines have a greater interest, in that they establish
with delicate sureness the relationship of the dandy with the orthodox moral
judges. The assessments of Mrs. Erlynne by the Windermeres are both wide
of the mark. For the husband she is simply a good strategist; for his wife

she is virtuous. She is in fact, up to a point, both. But the important fact is that her strategy is bound up with self-sacrifice in a way that Windermere does not recognize, while her virtue is quite other than Lady Windermere imagines it to be. Her behaviour in fact cannot be described exclusively in terms of either artifice or ethics. Her future husband too is satisfied that she has "explained every demmed thing"; but she has really done nothing of the sort. Rather she has built out of her conduct a beautiful, false image of herself, which will give pleasure to Lady Windermere and sustain the couple's happpiness. Her behaviour is seen as a praiseworthy and effective embodiment of the dandy's aspiration to turn his own life into a work of art, and recalls the Wildean dictum that "lying, the telling of beautiful, untrue things, is the proper aim of Art." But in the play as a whole this "proper aim" is only fitfully achieved, and behind the successful conclusion lie unresolved moral and aesthetic tensions.

If the dandy as lover causes difficulty in *Lady Windermere's Fan,* the dandy as villain in *A Woman of No Importance* (1893) causes considerably more. It would seem that Wilde had not yet grasped the fatal significance of making his dandy into a character, equipped, in however simple a way, with complexity of motive and a capacity for involvement in emotional affairs. By nature a bystander, the dandy is forced in these first two plays to become a participant, and confusion results. In Darlington's case he was at least cast favourably in both roles; in Illingworth's, it seems, we have to admire him in one and dislike him in the other.

"The world says that Lord Illingworth is very, very wicked," remarks Lady Stutfield. And Illingworth rejoins: "But what world says that, Lady Stutfield? It must be the next world. This world and I are on excellent terms." Unfortunately for Wilde's play it is neither Lady Stutfield nor the next world that judges Illingworth to be wicked, but Mrs. Arbuthnot, the central character and, from one point of view, the heroine of the play. Wooed by Illingworth in the past, she was promised marriage and then deserted and left to bring up her child without any support. She now finds herself again in Illingworth's social circle, and her son has just been offered the prospect of a successful career as his private secretary. Indifferent to the situation of the mother, patronizing to her son, flirtatious towards the girl with whom the boy is in love—the moral case against Illingworth is a strong one, and Lady Stutfield's remark, for all its archness, points to a reality. But if Illingworth is the villain of the piece, he is also, for long stretches, its hero. His intelligence, vitality, and wit make the rest of the characters seem anaemic. If he can show up the triviality and malice of the social set which surrounds him, he is equally capable of making us sense the rigidity and self-satisfaction behind Hester's puritan values and Mrs. Arbuthnot's religiose grief. And yet this superiority of attitude seems to exist quite apart from the moral situation in which he finds himself. This has nothing to do with complexity of character—it is not that kind of play; it arises from an ambiguity in his conception. If we look at Illingworth more carefully we shall see that this "superiority" does not belong to him in propria persona; it is the author temporarily speaking through him. When it comes to advancing the plot, however, Wilde has as it were to desert Illingworth and think of him in the wicked role in which he has cast him. The more Illingworth moves into the plot, the less Wilde cares about what he says; so that his final lines, as he leaves Mrs. Arbuthnot, have all the clichés of phrase and attitude of the stock-in-trade villain:

> Quarter to two! Must be strolling back to Hunstanton. Don't suppose I shall see you there again. I'm sorry, I am, really. It's been an amusing experience to have met amongst people of one's own rank, and treated quite seriously too, one's mistress and one's.

It seems quite fitting that Illingworth's stagey words should be brought to an end by a melodramatic gesture—and Mrs. Arbuthnot duly "snaches up glove and strikes Lord Illingworth across the face with it." This routine melodramatic finale suggests how little Wilde's attention is really engaged with the moral questions which is plot genuinely seems to raise. Justice has to be done to Mrs. Arbuthnot, but it is enough for Wilde if it is seen to be done. The center of his interest remains in the dandy and in trying to realize the significance of the dandy in an appropriate action. In *Lady Windermere's Fan* he had become a sympathetic lover and had been rendered null; in *A Woman of No Importance* he has been a faithless lover and is degraded into a melodramatic villain.

Involvement of one kind or another was the root defect of these plays, and in writing this third play, *An Ideal Husband* (1895), Wilde seems to have taken special care to keep his dandy free from commitment. If Lord Goring is to be in love it will be with a minor figure of the play, and his "love" will simply be there to testify to his status as hero. His connection with the central figures of the play will not be a profoundly emotional one, and will not involve him with a woman, faithfully or otherwise. And so we find Wilde giving Goring a friendship with Sir Robert Chiltern and hoping that the dandy, limited to the more fitting role of guide and philosopher, will at last find insurance against loss of wit.

Connected with Wilde's clearer insight into the dramatic requirements of the dandy was his decision to make the central plot of *An Ideal Husband* much wider, much more public in concern, than that of the earlier plays. Here, for the first and only time, a man's profession is central to the play. If Lady Chiltern demands an ideal husband this is intimately connected with the requirement that he must be an ideal politician. Corruption in the one sphere is, for her, corruption in the other.

This, then, is the world that faces the dandy; and now Wilde introduces him to us:

> Enter Lord Goring. Thirty-four, but always says he is younger. A well-bred, expressionless face. He is clever, but would not like to be thought so. A flawless dandy, he would be annoyed if he were considered romantic. He plays with life, and is on perfectly good terms with the world. He is fond of being misunderstood. It gives him a post of vantage.

It is from this post of vantage that he sees an eminent politician being blackmailed, because of a past misdeed, into supporting a political scheme which he considers fraudulent; he sees his vain attempts to keep this from his wife, and her reactions when she learns the truth. At critical moments he is appealed to for help, and through his successful intervention the plot is happily resolved.

For the first time Wilde gives us a satisfactory portrait of the dandy. Unlike Darlington's and Illingworth's it is not a portrait confused by the plot. In Goring we feel that Wilde can use his own voice and remain confident that the character is appropriate to the play. But it is an appropriateness that has a significant limitation. This is a play of political intrigue, of action; and such intrigue, such action, are alien to the dandy. It is interesting to note how Wilde overcomes the difficulties which ensue. Goring has two decisive actions in the play. The first, his thwarting of Mrs. Cheveley's plans of blackmail, is made possible by his finding a bracelet which she has lost and which he knows to have been stolen. The blackmailer become blackmailed. It is a significantly arbitrary device, too casually introduced by Wilde. Goring is lucky enough to be in a position to expose Mrs. Cheveley. But it is good fortune which has nothing to do with his specific role as "the first well-dressed philosopher in the history of thought." Goring's second crucial action is to persuade Lady Chiltern to allow her husband to remain in public life and accept the seat in the cabinet which has just been offered him. And this takes the form of a set speech, in Wilde's characteristic anti-puritanical manner, prefaced by a stage-direction to the effect that Goring here shows "the philosopher that underlies the dandy."

The action is not really resolved in dramatic terms; it is arrested, and dialectic is allowed to demolish the plot. But as Goring is inseparable from Wilde, this dialectic simply belongs to the author, and clearly it must end in victory. Goring resolves the problems in the play, certainly, but this is because Wilde has endowed him with an effortless superiority over everyone else. In Goring, then, Wilde has found an appropriate dramatic voice for himself, but he has not found a world where that voice can have a really appropriate dramatic effect.

However lightly it may be sketched in, the world of *An Ideal Husband* is a world where ambition and disgrace, love and suspicion, are possible. It is, uniquely in Wilde, a world of work. From his post of vantage the dandy may observe keenly and comment shrewdly, but he can never affect this world except through the arbitrary good fortune which the author has conferred on him. On his won, Goring is Wilde's most successful dandy; in the Chiltern-Cheveley world he is a wraith, lucky enough to be his author's Scarlet Pimpernel. His father's constant rebuke that he is wasting his time is not so easily dismissed as Wilde would like us to think.

It seems reasonable to think that, in creating a dandy satisfactorily, even though in isolation, Wilde was beginning to realize precisely the dramatic action he required. There are significant stage-directions in the third act. The first refers to a completely minor character, Goring's butler:

> The distinction of Phipps is his impassivity. He has been termed by enthusiasts the Ideal Butler. The Sphinx is not so incommunicable. He is a mask with a manner. Of his intellectual or emotional life history knows nothing. He represents the dominance of form.

The second refers to Goring:

> One sees that he stand in immediate relation to modern life, *makes it indeed, and so masters it*. (my italics)

In these two directions we find, indicated abstractly, the solution to the problem that has dogged Wilde's progress as a dramatist. Repeatedly the dandy has been broken on the wheel of the everyday world, sometimes too involved a figure, sometimes incapable of being involved enough. And now Wilde begins to see that, if the dandy is to master the world, it can be only a world of his own making. Only in a *world* of dandies will his voice and actions become harmonious: a world where the categories of serious and frivolous will no longer apply, where every character can speak like the author and the author like every character, where everything that can be seen in harmonious and there is nothing that cannot be seen. The dandy can exist fully only in a world of idyll, of pure play. And at last, in *The Importance of Being Earnest* (1895), he finds himself in such a world.

II

The prevalence of cant is a constant target for Wilde, and a topic which receives significant mention in three of his four plays is the varying attitudes taken up by—and towards—men and women in matters of sexual morality. It is there in Hester's upholstered rhetoric in *A Woman of No Importance:*

> If a man and woman have sinned, let them both go forth into the desert to love or loathe each other there. Let them both be branded. Set a mark, if you wish, on each, but don't punish the one and let the other go free. Don't have one law for men and another for women.

More coolly, it is there in Lord Darlington's exchange with Lady Windermere:

> LORD DARLINGTON: Do you think seriously that women who
> have committed what the world calls a fault should never
> be forgiven?
> LADY WINDERMERE: I think they should never be forgiven.
> LORD DARLINGTON: And men? Do you think that there should
> be the same laws for men as there are for women?
> LADY WINDERMERE: Certainly!
> LORD DARLINGTON: I think life too complex a thing to be
> settled by these hard and fast rules.

And then we find it again towards the end of *The Importance of Being Earnest:*

> JACK: Unmarried! I do not deny that is a serious blow. But
> after all, who has the right to cast a stone against one
> who has suffered? Cannot repentance wipe out an act of
> folly? Why should there be one law for men, and another
> for women? Mother, I forgive you.

The most cursory reading, of course, reveals that, however similar these passages may be, the last one is markedly different in tone from the other two. And it is this difference in tone which constitutes the essential difference between *Earnest* and the plays which preceded it. It is a tone which emerges as a result of sentiments from widely different contexts being fused together into a single statement. Beginning with mock-understatement—"I do not deny that is a serious blow"—it moves on through biblical reference to the clichés of romantic melodrama. The effect of this on the audience is to maintain a complete moral disengagement. But though Wilde's tone cuts out any ethical response to the sentiment, it makes completely real a character and a world where the sentiment seems quite appropriate. In other words, if we are kept deliberately disengaged from ever thinking of Jack's world as our own, we are kept no less deliberately engaged, by seeing the reality of Jack's world for *him*.

In the earlier plays, as we have seen, the reality of the dandy's world crumbled at the point where he became involved in the dramatic action. Now, in *Earnest,* at the height of the dramatic action, Jack's world is still perfectly viable. This testifies to Wilde's complete success in finding, in this play, the appropriate context for the dandy, and it is a characteristic touch of bravura that the testimony consists in making sustained play with the very situation which had earlier taken such toll of the dandy. We are now in a position to describe directly how Wilde has succeeded in finding a world fit for dandies to live in.

Everything starts from language. The characteristic language of the dandy is the paradox, and the essence of paradox is contradiction. This draws attention to two things—the attitude or sentiment which the paradox is concerned to reverse, and the language itself in which the reversal is done. We should say of paradox that it is a form of expression which is at once critical and self-delighting. And the same definition would apply very well to *Earnest* as a whole. Wilde is able to achieve this extension and uniformity because in this play the language of the dandy is a language appropriate to everyone. In the earlier plays, where the dandy was a figure involved with others who were not dandies, his idiom belonged to him in a very personal way: we were driven to reflect on *his* criticism, *his* self-delight. But when all the characters can speak with the author's voice they are completely insulated against each other; the criticism is then cut free to apply to a world beyond the characters, to the world of the audience. And in their turn the audience cannot think of any of the characters critically, because the delighting, and self-delighting, form of paradox creates a comic response which encloses these characters in a protective shell. Something of the way this works can be seen from the opening lines of the play; Algernon, who has been playing the piano in the next room, comes in and addresses his servant:

> ALGERNON: Did you hear what I was playing, Lane?
> LANE: I didn't think it polite to listen, sir.

This reveals, with splendid economy, the nature of the relationships between the characters in this play. The dandy, characteristically playing the piano and delighting in his own art, asks his servant for approval. Lane's reply is interesting. Taken in isolation it is the archetypal expression of deference from servant to master. Taken in this particular context it is of course the reverse: Lane is exercising his liberty to refuse to say what Algy expects from a servant on such an occasion. But when we take the question and answer *together,* we think neither of Algy's request nor of Lane's skillfully evasive reply, and what this may imply about them as people; we think simply of the perfect way in which they encounter each other. In other words we think of expression, of form, of the manner in which Wilde reveals the perfect servant as one who is the equal of his master.

If, at the end of the play, we are left thinking more of the dramatist than of his creation, this is not because of a personal intrusiveness—indeed, if this were so, the play would hardly have succeeded; but rather because of the precise rhetorical means through which Wilde has obtained and controlled our attention. The use of striking linguistic display, such as paradox, instantly draws attention to the author as manipulator; it is a reminder that words are man-made things. In realistic drama the author works in the opposite way: everything is done to give the impression that the characters are autonomous; the writer puts his skill into re-creating exact speech rhythms, idiosyncratic turns of phrase. The same is true in the realm of plot. The realistic dramatist will try to follow out as faithfully as possible the subtle configurations of daily life; Wilde finds his ideal plot in farce, because he sees art as exaggeration, and "selection, which is the very spirit of art, is nothing more than an intensified mode of over-emphasis." Nothing is more over-emphatic than farce, permitting as it does the maximum of coincidence and unlikelihood. Paradox in language, farce in plot—these are Wilde's chief resources in directing our response away from the characters and towards the play. Because for him it is in the play as such, embodying an imaginative world of perfect harmony, that life, "so terribly deficient in form," is given a meaning. Before exploring this, it is worth looking more exactly at the elements of farce and character in *Earnest.*

One of the ways in which Wilde defines his conception of plot and character is by making the characters themselves take on the role of plot-makers. They will shape their lives with the same complete confidence as they shape their phrases. So we find act 1 opening with Jack playing the part of Ernest and coming up to town to woo Gwendolen, and closing with Algernon playing the part of Ernest and going down to the country to woo Cecily. In the second act Algernon appears as Ernest and Jack as Ernest's bereaved brother. The girls dramatize their lives in their diaries and plan to marry not the right man, but the right name—Ernest. Eventually the mythical plot takes over and is shown to be "truer" than the real plot—Jack is, in fact, Ernest. Plot-makers of this sort can never be taken by surprise, they feel too sure of themselves for that. And consequently, at the times when things appear to be going wrong—Lady Bracknell's refusal to let Gwendolen marry Jack, Algernon's appearance as Ernest at the moment when Jack is mourning his death, the girls' discovery that "Ernest" is a fiction—no one is abashed; there is just a momentary pause and new resources of plot are immediately called upon. Shaw found the play "inhuman" and of course, in a sense, he was right: Wilde's whole art is calculated to prevent his characters' becoming people. If they did, they could no longer say perfectly all they have to say, they could no longer act as the masters of fortune, they could no longer cooperate with the author in validating the truth of his world, a truth founded not in reality but in imaginative cohesiveness, a truth sensed in shape.

Whenever the plot seems to be moving towards reality we see language taking it over and designing it into fantasy. There is, for example, the love scene in act 1, which culminates like this:

> GWENDOLEN: We live, as I hope you know, Mr. Worthing, in an age of ideals. The fact is constantly mentioned in the more expensive monthly magazines, and has reached the provincial pulpits, I am told; and my ideal has always been to love someone of the name of Ernest. There is something in that name that inspires absolute confidence. The moment Algernon first mentioned to me that he had a friend called Ernest, I knew I was destined to love you.
> JACK: You really love me, Gwendolen?
> GWENDOLEN: Passionately!
> JACK: Darling! You don't know how happy you've made me.
> GWENDOLEN: My own Ernest!

It is a splendid climax, perfectly appropriate for the "love scene," and at the same time perfectly undercutting its reality. When Jack goes on to hint that his name might not be Ernest, Gwendolen dismisses the suggestion briskly as having "very little reference at all to the actual facts of life, as we know them"—another ironical gloss on the question of reality.

Lady Bracknell is interesting in that we do feel, here, that we have in a quiet ordinary sense of the word a "character." But she too builds up her whole mode of speech out of bemusing herself with her own voice. If she exists at all, it is in an echochamber. She is so used to speaking in tones of imperious command that these persist regardless of what she is talking about:

> Well, I must say, Algernon, that I think it is high time that Mr. Bunbury made up his mind whether he was going to live or to die. This shilly-shallying with the question is absurd. Nor do I in any way approve . . . I consider . . . I am always telling . . . etc., etc.

It is not only her own tone that hypnotizes her, it is often a phrase itself: "But German sounds a thoroughly respectable language, and indeed, I believe, is so." The first rather curious statement gets a splendid endorsement from the would-be pedantic accuracy of the second.

A good example of "serious" situation, tone, and individual phrase combining together in this process of de-realization occurs when Jack arrives dressed in his mourning clothes:

> CHASUBLE: Dear Mr. Worthing, I trust this garb of woe does not betoken some terrible calamity?
> JACK: My brother.
> MISS PRISM: More shameful debts and extravagance?
> CHASUBLE: Still leading his life of pleasure?
> JACK (shaking his head): Dead!
> CHASUBLE: Your brother Ernest dead?
> JACK: Quite dead.
> MISS PRISM: What a lesson for him! I trust he will profit by it.

It is a rich exchange. Chasuble, reacting automatically to black, goes into his trade language—"garb of woe," "betoken," "terrible calamity." One routine response fades and is immediately replaced by another, "Still leading his life of pleasure?"—which is an odd hypothesis as to why Jack should be in mourning. It is after "pleasure" that Jack drops his monosyllable, "dead." Chasuble, still in the same mechanically solicitous tone, repeats, "Your brother Ernest dead?" Jack then returns his splendidly superfluous "quite dead." Interspersed with these exchanges are those of Miss Prism, who is as eccentrically unresponsive to the situation as Chasuble is eccentrically responsive. The effect of this triple play—Jack solemnly in mourning for a fiction, the other two quite incapable of making an appropriate response to the announcement—is to make form everything and content nothing. The interesting point that emerges from looking at this passage is that here Wilde is exercising his linguistic control for a purpose very different from the one revealed in the Jack-Gwendolen passage which we looked at earlier. There, the rhetorical situation kept feeling at bay, it was impossible to think of the scene as either passionate or heartless; now the rhetoric keeps farce at bay. The fact that Ernest is a fictitious character, and that Jack is solemnly arrayed in mourning for him, certainly goes far towards creating a *merely* farcical situation; but Wilde's scrupulous attention to the exact responses of Chasuble and Miss Prism keeps *our* attention, as always, on the language, rather than on the pure comedy of situation. Farce in Wilde is always shaped and controlled by precision of language, and it is this which distinguishes it from farce in general, which is shaped by arbitrariness of event.

The dramatic creation of the dandy, the creation of a world capable of projecting the dandy—we can see the problems involved in these undertakings, and we shall probably be willing to admit that *Earnest* solves them satisfactorily. But a question still remains about the nature of the success, a question which can be brought into sharper focus if we think of Wilde's play in relation to the comedies of other dramatists.

When we finish reading or seeing a play of Shakespeare's we are left thinking of the profound imaginative world which he has created; at the end of a Jonson play we can see how farce can bring to vivid life human vice and folly. But what are we left with at the end of *The Importance of Being Earnest?* There is here no "perilous stuff that weighs upon the heart," nor "sport that plays with follies, not with crimes." Eric Bentley attempts an answer to this question in *The Playwright as Thinker*. After commenting that nothing is easier than to handle this play without noticing what it contains, he goes on to exhibit its contents:

> The margins of an annotated copy of *The Importance of Being Earnest* would show such things as death, money, marriage, the nature of style, ideology and economics, beauty and truth, the psychology of philanthropy, the decline of aristocracy, nineteenth century morals, the class system. What begins as a prank ends as a criticism of life. What begins as intellectual high-kicking ends as intellectual sharpshooting.

This seems a misleading description because Bentley gives the impression of a play containing serious ideas which have been attractively packaged in wit. The best critic is he who opens the parcel most dextrously. But nothing, surely, is gained by recommending this play as if it were one of Shaw's. Yet again it is possible to see, only too clearly, Mr. Bentley's difficulty. Our vocabulary of approval is dominated by representational considerations like "truth to character," "truth to situation," or else by didactic ones like "social or moral vision." A dramatist who offers neither character nor social or moral vision would seem to be offering only triviality. What is it, then, which distinguishes *Earnest* from *Charley's Aunt?*

The difference, ultimately, is the same as that which distinguishes Shakespeare and Jonson from countless less successful dramatists, the use of language. But whereas their language was a means to an end, and their end conforms fairly directly with Johnson's definition of the function of literature—"to enable readers better to enjoy life or better to endure it," Wilde was concerned with the linguistic artifact itself, with a kind of poetry which Auden has described as "a verbal earthly paradise, a timeless world of pure play, which gives us delight because of its contrast to our historical existence with all its insoluble problems and inescapable suffering." To think of Wilde's art as merely "escapist" is to oversimplify the position. What he gives us is a completely realized idyll, offering itself as something irrevocably *other* than life, not a wish-fulfilment of life as it might be lived. Consequently, to think of Wilde's idyll in terms of "aspiration" or "rejection" is as idle as the notion of "accepting" or "rejecting" Keats's "Ode on a Grecian Urn," or the urn itself, or Mozart's "Marriage of Figaro." "Truth in art is the unity of a thing with itself," and the truth in Wilde's dictum can be falsified by art too self-consciously pursued, as well as by life. *Salome,* Wilde's last produced play, is a monument to art, not art itself; it is as entangled with an aesthetic commentary on life as *A Woman of No Importance* is with a moral one. *Earnest* is the dramatic expression of a precise aesthetic ideology, where Art is seen as the supreme ordering and perfection of life. In such a play the plot can never be our sort of plot, and so, in Wilde, it is a farce; the characters can never be human, and so, in Wilde, they are pure and simple; the language has to be our language, but if it is the language of paradox it can continually contradict us. Such a play can contain oblique criticism of life, but it will never be a direct imitation of life, since that would imply an intrinsic value in life superior to that of art. Even at its most topical *The Importance of Being Earnest* avoids the didactic and the narrowly satirical, and remains resolutely faithful to its aesthetic aim. It was a success which Wilde achieved only once, and we can feel reasonably certain that the sudden ending of his dramatic career did not deprive us of any better play.

Satire and Fantasy in Wilde's
The Importance of Being Earnest

Robert J. Jordan

The efforts of critics to rescue *The Importance of Being Earnest* from the triviality that Wilde claimed for it have led in recent years to two approaches. On the one hand Wilde's epigrammatic wit is analysed as an instrument of social criticism and the play is elevated to seriousness as a satire. On the other hand its fantasy is viewed as an expression of the author's aesthetic creed and so is accorded the dignity of a philosophy. The aim of this article is to consider aspects of both the satire and the fantasy, although the greater weight will be given to the latter as the more important of the two elements.

The form of wit that lends particular support to the claim of social significance is that used to describe Lady Harbury's widowhood, "I never saw a woman so altered; she looks quite twenty years younger." In such a comment the platitudinous phrases embodying some conventional sentiment on morality or social behaviour are taken, one or two words (preferably towards the end) are altered, and the whole thing is blown sky-high. A sense of security is created as the tired, familiar words roll out and then suddenly comes the jolt. Instead of the conventional sentiment comes, more often than not, its complete negation, and the shock is all the greater because this inversion of the platitude often sounds just as plausible a record of human attitudes as the platitude itself. Since the very existence of the cliché in the first place implies a standard and largely unquestioned attitude to the particular subject it deals with, this explosion of the cliché becomes an attack on the illusions and the hypocrisies of men.

From *Ariel* 1, no. 3 (July 1970). © 1970 by A. Norman Jeffares and the University of Calgary.

As a trick of speech this device, no matter how recurrent, is open to the criticism that it has merely an incidental role in the play. By its means, touches of satire appear in the dialogue but the overall fabric (the manoeuvres of the plot and the behaviour of the characters) is unaffected. It can be argued, however, in *The Importance of Being Earnest,* that the trick extends beyond the dialogue, for an analagous device does appear at the broader level. The most striking manifestation at this level is to be found in the treatment of the relationship of the sexes. In this play are two sophisticated young gentlemen and two respectable young ladies. The normal expectation is that the young ladies will be delicate, romantic, dependent, and the young men will be sufficiently practical and experienced in the ways of the world to act as protectors for the young ladies—that they will have all the talents that high society demands of the escorts for its young women. Moreover, such an expectation does not seem unwarranted. Jack's serious manner and Algy's slightly cynical, slightly rakish worldliness seem to confirm that in their different ways these young men will have this social masterfulness.

But these expectations are completely flouted. The refined young ladies turn out to be hardheaded, cold-blooded, efficient and completely self-possessed and the young gentlemen simply crumple in front of them. Jack attempts a proposal of marriage, fluffs it, and finds Gwendolen taking the whole proceeding out of his hands and telling him what to do. Algy arrives in the country to have a flirtation with a country innocent and finds himself peremptorily assigned a role as fiancé in a relationship that the lady has organized for herself. It is the expectation of both women that their loved ones will be called Ernest and on this issue they are completely inflexible. The men wilt before their determination and are forced to scuttle around looking for a way of satisfying them.

This inverted relationship is the norm of the play. It is repeated in the Chasuble-Prism relationship where Chasuble is completely passive, and Prism the (somewhat bumbling) pursuer. The clearest example, however, is provided by the predicament of Lord Bracknell who, of course, never appears—whose nonappearance is indeed fitting, almost symbolic, since he is practically a nonperson. He is the complete cypher, so dominated by his female relatives that Gwendolen can use the trick of the inverted platitude and describe him in the phrases that customarily justify the stay-at-home woman:

> Outside the family circle, papa, I am glad to say, is entirely unknown. I think that is quite as it should be. The home seems to me to be the proper sphere for the man. And certainly once

a man begins to neglect his domestic duties he becomes painfully effeminate, does he not?

We are taught that female submissiveness was one of the bulwarks of Victorian upper-middle-class society and here we see that article of faith being mocked as a sham. If the inverted platitude at the level of dialogue can be claimed as part of a satiric vision then so too can the comparable inversion in the very fabric of the play.

But even if this satiric device is structural in the play it can hardly be said to provide a satire of any great power. The main objection is that the particular inversion that is offered to us here is a commonplace of social criticism at the time the play was written. *The Importance of Being Earnest,* after all, is a product of the age of the New Woman—the suffrage movement, the rational clothes movement, women in sport, women at the universities and so on. If a journal such as *Punch* shows a consistent interest in "Oscar," "Daubaway Weirdsley" and the Decadence its concern with the New Woman could be said to be positively obsessive. There is not an issue in the 1894–95 period without some joke or comment on the subject and sometimes there are as many as half a dozen, most of them turning on the often objectionable forcefulness of the modern woman as opposed to the mere male. There is, for example, the cartoon of cowed and diminutive Tibbins whose wife has been asked to resign from the Omphale Club for ungentlemanly conduct, or the picture of a fine handsome young woman asking the elegant monocled young man if she might carry his bag for him, or verses such as the following, particularly interesting in relation to Lord Bracknell:

> MAMMA is a judge of divorces,
>   Sister ANNE is a learned Q.C.,
> ELIZA is great upon horses,
>   And DORA a thriving M.D.
> Aunt JANE is a popular preacher,
>   Aunt SUSAN a dealer in stocks,
> While Father, the gentlest old creature,
>   Attends to the family socks.
>
>   . . . .
>
> I'm to marry a girl in the City,
>   She allows me a hundred a year
> To dress on, and make myself pretty,
>   And keep me in baccy and beer.
> The duties?—Oh, as for the duties,

> You can possibly guess what they are;
> And I warrant the boys will be beauties
> That are destined to call me Papa.

In the case of Gwendolen, moreover, we appear to have not only this general situation but also specific echoes of the New Woman. Gwendolen apparently attends university extension lectures and she talks glibly of "metaphysical speculations" and "German scepticism" so that Jack, who is in some awe of her, can speak of her as an "intellectual girl." This erudition, together with her cold masterfulness, strongly suggests the standard satire on one variety of the New Woman.

Social criticism, then, though it is present in the action as well as the dialogue of the play, is still of no great power. In spite of it the heart of the work is elsewhere. If at one level the play is a social satire and at another it is a farce, at the most important level it seems to be a fantasy in which unattainable human ideals are allowed to realize themselves.

The most obvious ideal presented in the play is the dream of elegance, of effortlessly achieved grace and formal perfection. The aspiration here is stated explicitly in a whole series of paradoxes in which form or style is elevated above truth or virtue, notably in the exchange in the first few minutes of act 3. It is realized dramatically in the delicate symmetry of the plot, with its balanced characters and situations, and in the polish of the dialogue and the elegant chiselling of the epigrams. Many of these epigrams may use social comment as their material but it can be argued that in such cases the brilliance of the effect is ultimately more striking than the pungency of the criticism.

This element in the play has been much analysed, especially in relation to the cult of the dandy and the aesthetic creed that underlies him. There is, however, another aspect of the idealization. One of the things about the world of the play is its innocence. This is a world many of whose characters seem completely indifferent to morality, but at the same time it is a world without evil. The absence of a moral sense, then, does not let loose sin and degradation, because to a large extent these things do not exist, except as unemotional abstractions. Miss Prism may have to warn her charge not to read certain "sensational" parts of a book but what endangers Cecily in this innocent world is not corrupting sexual outspokenness. It is the fallen Rupee, not the fallen woman, that threatens to disturb her.

Now if the play's opening situation were being treated realistically, innocence is one of the last things to be expected, for what we are presented with are two young men who are leading double lives, lives of outward social conformity coupled with lives devoted to secret pleasures. In the normal course of things this would almost inevitably imply sexual licence cloaked by Victorian hypocrisy, and at least two of the standard centres for the gentleman debauchee, Paris and the Empire Music Hall, receive passing mention in the text. But whatever the normal expectation the behaviour of Jack and Algy that we actually witness is infinitely removed from this world of sexual corruption. By taking up the "secret life" pattern the play is in a sense flirting with the possibilities of sex but when it comes to the point all such areas of experience are rigorously excluded. We watch as Algy goes on what might well be a sexual adventure, his descent on Jack's country house, but what results is completely innocuous.

However, while Algy may be a sexual innocent, he does reveal appetite in another form. In act 1 he indulges himself with an entire plate of cucumber sandwiches, and in act 2 the barrier breaks again and he wolfs the greater part of a plate of muffins. The role of this food-lust as a vice appears more clearly in the four-act version of the play where Dr Chasuble declares that Jack should not pay "Ernest's" supper debts because it "would be encouraging his profligacy," while Miss Prism, having declared on the same page that "There can be little good in any young man who eats so much, and so often," later remarks that "to partake of two luncheons in one day would not be liberty. It would be licence." In a sense, then, Algy is lustful, but his lust is innocence itself.

This innocent vice does, however, suggest something. It is the vice, the wickedness of the child. Algernon is the naughty little boy who eats all the goodies. And in this lies a clue to this innocence which is central to the play as fantasy. All the young people are terribly elegant, exquisitely sophisticated adults. But much of their behaviour and many of their attitudes are redolent of the world of the child.

Consider, for example, Cecily. To begin with, we first hear of her as "little Cecily" who has given a present to her dear uncle. Then, when we first meet her it is in the presence of her governess. It is quite possible that a girl of her age would still be studying under a private tutor, but uncle, tutor and the adjective little all suggest something of the child. Furthermore the main impression that is made in that scene in which we first see her is that little Cecily doesn't like school. As she herself expresses it, "Horrid Political Economy! Horrid Geography! Horrid, horrid German." Added to this somewhat stage-juvenile mode of expression is the fact that she cannot spell "cough" and indeed, that the letters she had written to herself were all badly spelled. It can also be argued that her impatience and the way it is expressed is evocative of the child. At the prospect of having to wait seventeen years to marry she declared, "I couldn't wait all that time. I hate waiting even five minutes for anybody. It always makes me rather cross."

In Cecily's case the childlike qualities are omnipresent. Elsewhere they are not so persistent, but if this idea of the characters as child-adults is considered, a point of reference may be found for many of their most characteristic responses. Much of the quarrelling in the play, for example, has the quality of children's tiffs, and a childlike petulance is a recurrent note. It is illustrated in the lovers' quarrel at the end of act 2 and the beginning of act 3, while the petulance by itself is perfectly revealed at the end of act 1 where we see Jack and Algy trying to decide how they will amuse themselves that evening:

> ALGERNON: What shall we do after dinner? Go to a theatre?
> JACK: Oh, no! I loathe listening.
> ALGERNON: Well, let us go to the Club?
> JACK: Oh, no! I hate talking.
> ALGERNON: Well, we might trot round to the Empire at ten?
> JACK: Oh, no! I can't bear looking at things. It is so silly.
> ALGERNON: Well, what shall we do?
> JACK: Nothing!
> ALGERNON: It is awfully hard work doing nothing.

This is extraordinarily like the cliché of a spoilt child sulkily refusing to play the various games suggested by a friend. Indeed, children's games are evoked by a whole series of features in the play. A significant part of the action is the playing of "pretend" games—Algy's Bunbury, Jack's Ernest, Cecily's fiancé—all involving imaginary characters who can, if need be, be killed off when they begin to get in the way of the game. There is also a great concern with the rules of the game—Algy insisting on telling Jack how to play Bunburying, Gwendolen instructing Jack how to propose properly, Cecily insisting on the correct forms and procedures from Algy. Moreover not only because of these games but also because of the general attitude to life the one sin that is more frequent in the play than gluttony is the equally childish one of "telling fibs." When Jack makes his grave charges against Algy's moral character to Lady Bracknell this is the substance of them, and yet earlier Jack himself had been made to squirm when caught out in a major lie—indicating at the time that lying was his unvarying practice. Throughout the play there is a scattering of bland falsehoods on minor issues (the unavailability of cucumbers, little Aunt Cecily of Tunbridge Wells) and there is always, of course, the series of paradoxes referred to earlier, in which the stylish lie is said to be preferable to the truth. In view of all these intimations of childhood, then, it is significant that some of the broader jokes in the play spring directly from the involvement of the characters in childish situations—the preoccupation with christening, for example, or Jack rushing into the arms of Miss Prism with a cry of "mother."

Of course not everybody in the play has these qualities of the child. Lady Bracknell, for example, is very much the adult—the person of irresistible authority and power who interrupts the games to demand what is going on. Jack in particular is in complete awe of her and looks on her as the immensely older person—to him she is someone who must be well over one hundred and fifty. The other adults in the play are Chasuble and Miss Prism, the latter being for a few fleeting seconds Jack's mother. With these two, adulthood is characterized partly by authority and age but much more so by the way the aura of innocence does not extend to them. Their conversation, particularly in the scene in which they are first established on stage, is marked by its uneasy undertones of sexuality—"hang upon her lips," "metaphor . . . drawn from bees," "young women are green." Indeed Miss Prism's pointed reference to an unmarried man as a "permanent public temptation" cannot even be dismissed as an undertone.

There is, then, an atmosphere of innocence and freedom from corruption in this play that is in part created by insinuations of the childlike into the manners and attitudes of the characters. The child as embodiment of innocence and of the creative imagination is one of the obsessive nineteenth-century symbols and that Wilde himself has an interest in the world of children is implied in his experiments with the fairy-tale as a literary form. It might even be possible to claim that the element of the childlike in this play is an extension of the cult of youth that is a significant part of his thinking and that dictates sayings such as "The condition of perfection is idleness: the aim of perfection is youth." In any case children have a quality apart from their innocence that might well recommend them to Wilde, their ability to approach their own fantasies and their own trivial pastimes with intense gravity and seriousness. Part of the play's philosophy, after all, is allegedly that "we should treat all the trivial things of life seriously."

In this analysis of the play's fantasy two strands, elegance and innocence, have been distinguished. In fact they are not without relevance to one another. The perfection of elegance is best achieved in the absence of strong human emotion or of moral intensity since the presence of such fervour is likely to ruffle the elegance or make it appear, by comparison, trivial and futile. The pint-sized passions of Wilde's characters (petulance, hunger, impatience), together with their lack of moral concern thus create an atmosphere congenial to the flowering of the sophisticated manner. But at the same time some down-to-earth awareness of the tensions or weaknesses of humanity can serve a useful purpose in such a context and it is here that the social satire, the material of much of the elegant wit, has its place in the fantasy world. This conjunction of mild satire and fantasy in fact represents a fairly basic piece of literary tact. It enables the author to have his fantasy and at the same time to indicate his awareness of the imperfection of the world as it really is, to prevent the charge of naiveté by demonstrating an acute sense of things as they are and to brace the self-indulgence by surrounding it with laughter.

Oscar Wilde's Great Farce:
The Importance of Being Earnest

David Parker

It is generally agreed that *The Importance of Being Earnest* is Oscar Wilde's masterpiece, but there is little agreement on why it should be thought so or on how it works as a play. Though we can sense a solid substance beneath the frothy surface, the nature of that substance remains an enigma. Surprisingly little real criticism has been written about the play, and much of that which has is sketchy or tedious. One of the few critics whose mind seems to have been genuinely engaged by the play is Mary McCarthy, but she has written about it only briefly, and despite her admiration clearly finds it repugnant. "It has the character of a ferocious idyll," she says, and complains that "Selfishness and servility are the moral alternatives presented." Most of what she says about the play cannot be denied, yet there is a wrong note somewhere. Though it is almost always feeble to complain about critics using the wrong standards, I think we have to do so here. *The Importance of Being Earnest* does not tackle problems of moral conduct in the way that most plays do. In it, Wilde expresses a comic vision of the human condition by deliberately distorting actuality and having most of the characters behave as if that vision were all but universal. It is fair enough to complain about the vision entire, but to complain simply about the selfishness, without asking what it suggests, is on a par with complaining about the immorality of *Tom Jones*.

Though McCarthy uses the wrong standards, and therefore sees the play through a distorting lens, what she sees is there and needs to be studied.

From *Modern Language Quarterly* 35, no. 2 (June 1974). © 1974 by the University of Washington.

Her notion about the play's advocacy of selfishness may be got into better focus if we compare it with what William Empson says about the heroes of Restoration comedy: "There is an obscure paradox that the selfish man *is* the generous one, because he is not repressed, has 'good nature,' and so on." This seems to represent more accurately what goes on in Wilde's play, if only because it resembles Wilde's own way of thinking. Moreover, the play clearly owes something to the Restoration comic tradition. "My duty as a gentleman," says Algy, "has never interfered with my pleasures in the smallest degree," thus neatly summing up the principles by which the young bloods of Restoration comedy lived. They were understood to be gentlemen because they were Natural Men, responsive to impulse, capable of falling in love, and so on, in contrast to the inhibited, conventional, rule-obeying, theory-loving tradesmen, Puritans, and pedants, whom they despised. The heroes of Restoration comedy have been criticized too, often with justice, but one thing should be clear by now: their roguishness, their carelessness about money and sexual behavior, was presented not simply to be admired as such. These things had symbolic value as well. The suggestion was that aristocratic young men needed to abandon conventional morality and get back to basic impulse, if the values they represented (moral independence, for example) were not to be annihilated by commercialism and Puritanism. Their roguishness was a proof of freedom, as well as an excuse for scourging the bourgeoisie. Algy's selfishness, and that of the other characters, demands a similar interpretation. It has a satirical force, of course: the manners of the upper classes are being laughed at; but there is more to it than that. In Wilde's vision, a sort of honorable selfishness becomes not merely a virtue, but a moral sine qua non.

Wilde's play, it seems to me, is more successful than most Restoration comedies because it is more pure—more purely absurd, if you like. The process of distorting actuality for expressive purposes is carried out more thoroughly, and the play's moral and aesthetic integrity is better maintained. In the dialogue alone, there is a more consistent heightening, amounting to a transfiguration of everyday conversation. The trouble with many Restoration comedies is that they express values only half-believed in by the audience for which they were intended. The characters praise aristocratic recklessness and sneer at commerce, yet the original courtly audience was committed to, and dependent on, commerce for at least a large part of its wealth. As a result, because of a secret uncertainty in the playwrights, there is often a confusion between symbolic action and action seriously recommended to the audience for imitation. We are presented with hyperbolic actions and sentiments, which we find not entirely convincing and perhaps a shade hysterical. There is the standard paradox of Restoration comedy, for instance: all moralists are hypocrites; only libertines can see the truth and maintain a fundamental decency. The confusion carried over into real life. Many of the court wits and gallants tried to live out such paradoxes, not always with happy results. Wilde too tried to live out his own paradoxes, with decidedly unhappy results, but in his greatest play artifice and advice do not get mixed up. "I don't quite like women who are interested in philanthropic work," says Cecily. "I think it is so forward of them." This is funnier, and more percipient, than jokes about hypocritical Puritan tradesmen. Wilde's symbol for sensual vitality and obedience to impulse is itself more wisely chosen than that of the Restoration playwrights: instead of using sexual behavior, he uses eating, something much more easily distanced. Contrary to what McCarthy says, *The Importance of Being Earnest* rarely slips over into recommending attitudes that are morally repellent—relative to Restoration comedy, at any rate. You have to stand a long way off from the play to be able to think so. It is difficult to get indignant with the characters.

The farcical structure helps distance what we see, and Wilde exploits it in other ways too. Farce is not necessarily trivial, and even when it is, through its very nature it usually makes assertions and raises questions about human identity; that is what makes the same situations enduringly popular. The hero of farce is usually a cunning rogue who, in order to gratify some impulse, spins an elaborate deception, which his victims seem constantly on the verge of exposing, so that he is constantly threatened with defeat, punishment, or humiliation. We admire the hero because he has the courage to obey his impulses and because his tricks render him protean—free from imposed identity. We despise his victims becauses they are prisoners of manners, which repress impulse and forbid deception. They seem narrow and timid. A more highly wrought and expressive sort of farce is that in which all (or most) of the protagonists are rogues, who compete to satisfy their impulses. The moral independence of the most versatile, the most protean, is endorsed by success. *The Importance of Being Earnest* belongs to that sort.

Moreover, Wilde consciously exploits the concern of farce with human identity. The joke in the title is often thought of as a mock-pompous piece of frivolity, but it is more than that. The play might as justly be named "The Importance of Being." The whole thing is comically addressed to the problem of recognizing and defining human identity; we are made to see wide significance in Jack's polite request, "Lady Bracknell, I hate to seem inquisitive, but would you kindly inform me who I am?" The pun on *earnest* and *Ernest* merely makes the title more suitably comic. Neither being earnest nor being Ernest is of much help when confidence is lost in the substantiality of human identity. The concern with identity is repeatedly underlined in the text of the play, where statements that seem superficially only to poke fun at upper-class frivolity continually edge the mind toward a contemplation of the insubstantiality of identity. "It isn't easy to be anything nowadays," complains Algy in the first act. "There's such a lot of beastly competition about." And only a few lines later, Gwendolen feels obliged to deny that she is perfect: "It would leave no room for developments, and I intend to develop in many directions."

More than most writers of farce, Wilde was conscious of this concern with identity, so natural to the form, and he uses it to express a preoccupation which the nineteenth century gave birth to, and the twentieth century cherishes. Lurking always in the depths of the play is a steady contemplation of Nothingness, of *le néant,* which is all the more effective for its being, in contrast to most of its manifestations, comic in mode. Instead of making Nothingness a pretext for despair, Wilde finds in it a challenge to the imagination. For him, Nothingness in human identity, in human claims to knowledge, in the organization of society, becomes a field to be tilled by the artist—by the artist in each of us.

In many ways a writer owing more to French than to English traditions, in this respect too Wilde shares a quality of vision with Flaubert, Villiers, Zola, Barbey d'Aurevilly, and Mallarmé. They differ from each other, of course, as Wilde differs from them, but in the vision of each, as Robert Martin Adams says, "The shell of personal identity collapses, the yolk of individuality is split. Even grossness is a form of transparency, even knowledge is a form of complicated and difficult ignorance (Flaubert)." Yet for Wilde this brings liberation, not despair. Though he has Algy complain about what we might call the epistemological complacency of the English, he has him do it gaily: "That is the worst of the English. They are always degrading truths into facts, and when a truth becomes a fact, it loses all its intellectual value."

If *The Importance of Being Earnest* looks back to the French nineteenth century it also looks forward to the twentieth century and the drama of the absurd. The plot is absurd, in an obvious sense, and many critics have argued that it should be dismissed as a Gilbertian fantasy. It seems to me, however, that it is important, in the negative way that plots are, in the drama of the absurd. Everyone responds to preposterous situations in a way that is crazily systematic, defending his responses with absurdly sententious generalizations. Besides being used as a symbol for sensual vitality, eating becomes a subject for absurd imperatives. Algy, for instance, declares that "One should always eat muffins quite calmly. It is the only way to eat them." People's behavior and sentiments act as a parody of the real world; such, it is suggested, is the nature of all action, all moralizing. But Wilde carries off this parody better than most of the playwrights whom we now describe as dramatists of the absurd. He is never obvious. His parody always works at two levels, which enrich each other: it pokes fun at the manners of a particular class, and it satirizes the human condition. To my knowledge, only Pinter and Albee do anything at all like this, with comparative success.

Nothingness is repeatedly evoked in the verbal texture of the play in a way that prefigures techniques of the drama of the absurd. Characters are always using words like *serious* and *nonsense* in a manner that sends out little ripples of significance. "If you don't take care," Jack warns Algy,

> JACK: your friend Bunbury will get you into a serious scrape
> some day.
> ALGERNON: I love scrapes. They are the only things that are
> never serious.
> JACK: Oh, that's nonsense, Algy. You never talk anything but
> nonsense.
> ALGERNON: Nobody ever does.

Serious was recognized as a canting expression in the nineteenth century. "No one knows the power," wrote "F. Anstey" in 1885, "that a single serious hairdresser might effect with worldly customers" (*OED*). Algy's quasi pun works as a protest against the importance attached by the Victorians to the very business of attaching importance (parodied more broadly in Miss Prism); for them, it is often apparent, this was a means of imposing form and stability on a world whose evanescence they half-suspected, a procedure of course unacceptable to Wilde. The joke is parallel to the one about *earnest.*

The play on the word *nonsense* expresses a sensibility that is recognizably modern, though it lacks the anguish that is now usually part of it. The sense of futility that arises out of the contemplation of Nothingness is felt only by those whose belief in human dignity requires support from a religious mythology, or a quasi-religious mythology, such as that subscribed to by many humanists. When his mind was at its most creative, Wilde felt no such need, willingly abandoning intellectual comfort and security for intellectual adventurousness in the unknown and unknowable. Algy's perception of universal nonsense is cheerful; it has the gusto of quick intelligence; and because it also works as a gibe at Algy's class, it has a quality of immediate practical shrewdness that makes it the more acceptable.

In the middle of the play, *absurd* itself is used repeatedly to evoke a sense of immanent Nothingness. Jack cannot understand how he should have a brother in the dining-room: "I don't know how it all means. I think it is perfectly absurd." Algy will not deny that he is Jack's brother: "It would be absurd." Jack says the same about the notion that Algy should lunch twice, and he thinks Algy's presence in the garden at Woolton "utterly absurd." Algy disagrees with the contention that he has no right to "Bunbury" at Woolton: "That is absurd. One has a right to Bunbury anywhere one chooses." Gwendolen and Cecily agree that it is "absurd to talk of the equality of the sexes."

These words are used in jokes and casual comments that do not stand out in the text and are likely to be delivered in a carelessly cynical manner, as bits of flimflam designed simply to gain the speaker a tactical advantage in the argument; but they crop up repeatedly and affect the whole flavor of the play.

The use of paradox performs the same function much more obviously. Each paradox is a sort of miniature stylistic enactment of the notion expressed in one of the boldest: "In matters of grave importance style, not sincerity, is the vital thing." This pokes fun at the beau monde, of course, but it also hints at an answer to the problems raised in the jokes about *earnest* and *serious*. Once belief in epistemological certainty is abandoned, style, liberally interpreted, is more important than sincerity. By imposing a consciously provisional order onto evanescent reality, it makes practical decisions possible. Paradox imposes this order in a particularly striking way. It confounds conventional notions about order, identity, and dissimilarity, synthesizing new orders out of the confusion it exposes. Far from concealing chaos and disharmony, it rejoices in them, embraces them courageously, and takes them as a challenge to human wit and ingenuity. Wilde's rapid sequences of paradox after paradox picture for us a world in which men make, undo, and remake reality with almost every sentence they utter.

Of course, not all the paradoxes in *The Importance of Being Earnest* are purely verbal or confined to one remark. There is a sustained effort in the play to dissolve conventional notions of order in fields where they tend to hypertrophy. Wilde depicts a world in which the socially endorsed certainties are continually evaporating; values respecting social class, education, the Church, money, love, and the family undergo constant metamorphosis. Attitudes toward the family, in particular, are grotesquely transformed.

Algy cheerfully dismisses the sentiments associated with kinship: "Relations are simply a tedious pack of tedious people, who haven't got the remotest knowledge of how to live, nor the smallest instinct about when to die. Others invert the normal sentiments. Lady Bracknell speaks of an acquaintance whose husband has died: "I never saw a woman so altered, she looks quite twenty years younger." Gwendolen complains about her lack of influence over her mother: "Few parents nowadays pay any regard to what their children say to them! The old-fashioned respect for the young is rapidly dying out." She approves of her father's domestication, however: "The home seems to me to be the proper sphere for the man. And certainly once a man begins to neglect his domestic duties he becomes painfully effeminate, does he not?"

In plot and action, too, conventional notions about family life are broken down. The handbag in Jack's family history excites Lady Bracknell's famous protest: "To be born, or at any rate bred in a handbag, whether it had handles or not, seems to me to display a contempt for the ordinary decencies of family life that reminds one of the worst excesses of the French Revolution." The comedy is enhanced, of course, by the oddity of Lady Bracknell's own notions (or at least her way of expressing them). She seems to conceive family as something subject to human volition, and can advise Jack "to make a definite effort to produce, at any rate, one parent, of either sex, before the season is quite over." Though we may see parody of upper-class snobbery here, others do will relations into—and out of—existence, without there being any feeling of parody. Jack invents a brother; the girls invent ideal husbands. (Algy's Bunbury is only a friend, but the effect is much the same.) At the other extreme, the characters accept the family relationships revealed at the end of the play, with an absurd eagerness that is just as effective in ridiculing conventional notions. This is particularly evident in Jack's outburst, when he mistakenly assumes Miss Prism to be his mother. She indignantly reminds him that she is unmarried. "Cannot repentance wipe out an act of folly?" he cries. "Why should there be one law for men and another for women? Mother! I forgive you." The family is a category of everyday understanding that is one of the first to crumble before the vision of Nothingness. That is what enables Wilde's characters to adopt such a variety of postures with respect to it.

Individual identity, too, dissolves before the vision of Nothingness. That is why farce, and its traditional concern with human identity, was so useful to Wilde. Each character in *The Importance of Being Earnest* is a sort of vacuum that attains to individual identity only through an effort of the creative imagination. They are like Sartre's famous waiter in *L'Être et le néant,* except that they make their decisions consciously, and that we are pleased rather than nauseated by the process. Each attains to identity in the mode of *being what he is not.*

It is a sense of the insubstantiality of human identity which causes Wilde to place such emphasis on impulse (on selfishness, if you like). Admit all the problems of epistemology, and impulse still remains. Obedience to impulse is a defiant way of asserting some sort of basic identity. Algy's obsession with food is an example. "I hate people who are not serious about meals," he complains. "It is so shallow of them." Beneath the parody of manners, we can detect in this a perception, truthful within the terms of reference the play allows. Algy is prepared to use the word *serious* here because there is something fundamental to relate it to. When appetites are all that is substantial in human identity, all else must seem shallow. The two girls place a similar reliance on impulse. Both have faith in first impressions, and both are surprisingly candid about their sexual appetites. Cecily tells Algy, "I don't think you should tell me that you love me wildly, pasisonately, devotedly, hopelessly. Hopelessly doesn't seem to make much sense, does it?"

They are quick to change, though. When, after mutual declarations of devotion, Algy tells Cecily he will wait seventeen years for her hand, she replies, "Yes, I felt it instinctively. And I am so sorry for you, Algy. Because I couldn't wait all that time. I hate waiting even five minutes for anybody. It always makes me rather cross. I am not punctual myself, I know, but I do like punctuality in others, and waiting even to be married is quite out of the question." Changeability, in fact, is a corollary of obedience to impulse. As impulses vary, so must the attitudes of the individual. The protagonists of Wilde's play recognize this, particularly the girls. "I never change, except in my affections," Gwendolen announces. Their changeability is most amusingly demonstrated in the first meeting of Gwendolen and Cecily, when, in the course of a single scene, they proceed from mutual suspicion to mutual affection, thence to mutual detestation, and finally to mutual affection again, all the time firmly maintaining that they are consistent. The audience is likely to laugh at this sort of thing because it realizes that literary and social conventions are being ridiculed, but there is more to the comedy than that. There is a core of truth in what we are presented with: human beings do change. The joke lies in the way the characters are neither distressed nor surprised at their own changeability. In Wilde's world nothing else is expected.

Love might seem a surprising ingredient in such a world, but it is a play of courtship, and love does have importance in it. Love is based on impulse, after all, and for Wilde it is action, not object; a courageous creative effort of the will, not a substantial inner something; the free play of the imagination, not a faculty. The characters of the play constantly deny the substantiality of love, in speech and action. Their courtships consist in patterns of interlocking fantasy and wit; they woo through imposture and fancy; they pursue and fly; they test and torment each other. Never is there anything static or certain about their relationships. "The very essence of romance is uncertainty," says Algy. "If ever I get maried, I'll certainly try to forget the fact." Wilde is following Restoration comedy again, here. "Uncertainty and Expectation are the Joys of Life," says Congreve's Angelica. "Security is an insipid thing, and the overtaking and possessing of a Wish, discovers the Folly of the Chase." And as with Restoration comedy, we admire the lovers for their courage and their wit. We feel that they are absurd too (all action in the play is absurd; the secret is not minding), but at the same time we are made to feel that they are somehow right as well. The theme of sentimental education, normally found in romantic comedy, is parodied by inversion. Fantasies the lovers have about each other are confirmed rather than cured, almost as if wit, the creative imagination (call it what you will), were able magically to force the world into the shapes it suggests to itself. We feel, at any rate, that the lovers earn their partners by growing toward them, through wit.

Because the characters live in a world in which order is constantly vanishing, they scorn theory, consistency, and the appearance of simplicity. "The truth," as Algy says, "is rarely pure and never simple." Certainly, in matters of identity, seeming intelligibility is to be distrusted. "The simplicity of your nature," Gwendolen tells Jack, "makes you exquisitely incomprehensible to me." The characters are alert, not to a harmonious universal nature, but to a proliferation of separate, deceptive, and contradictory sense-impressions. Knowledge comes only through the imagination. Gwendolen laughs at Jack's misgivings over her delight in his being called (as she thinks) Ernest. He cautiously inquires how she might feel were his name not Ernest, but she will not listen. "Ah, that is clearly a metaphysical speculation," she says, "and like all metaphysical speculation, has very little reference at all to the actual facts of real life, as we know them." This is an ironic node. The observation by itself fits in with the general theme of the play, but in the immediate context the joke is against Gwendolen (and Jack, when we think how he must feel). He has only assumed the name of Ernest; her notions are just as "metaphysical"; and what seem to be the actual facts of real life thoroughly justify such a speculation. Yet at the end of the play, Gwendolen's faith in the name, her conviction that she will marry an Ernest, and her insistence that her lover conform to her ideal are all justified; we learn that Jack's true name is Ernest. One effect of all this is to satirize faith in ideals by having it vindicated absurdly, but there is more to it than that. We feel delighted at the outcome, not like the recipients of a warning. We are made to feel that confident fantasies justify themselves, that a bold imagination is more useful than plodding attention to apparent facts.

In Wilde's world truth itself dwindles into insignificance. The characters have a strictly practical attitude to the relationship between statements and actuality, the latter being so elusive. Charged with being named John, Jack declares, "I could deny it if I liked. I could deny anything if I liked." And he is embarrassed when required to utter things in strict correspondence with what seem to be facts: "It is very painful for me to be forced to speak the truth. It is the first time in my life that I have ever been reduced to such a painful position, and I am really quite inexperienced in doing anything of the kind, so you must excuse me if I stammer in my tale." He goes on to say that he has never had a brother, which turns out to be untrue; Algy is his brother. Once again the inference is that truth cannot be discovered through the senses and the intellect alone. Jack's witty lies are more percipient. The comic inversion of truth and untruth is maintained in Jack's dismay, when he learns that what he had thought to be lies are true. "Gwendolen," he says, "it is a terrible thing for a man to find out suddenly that all his life he has been speaking nothing but the truth. Can you forgive me?" She can. "There is always hope," she says, "even for those who are most accurate in their statements." Even when it is the art of living, we are tempted to gloss, "Lying, the telling of beautiful untrue things, is the proper aim of Art."

Jack and Algy certainly attain their ends through lying. They are true rogues, impulsive, lovers of deception and imposture. They fulfill themselves in the way of all rogues: by discovering human freedom in protean identity. Doubtless what they do permits us to laugh at the mad antics young gentlemen get up to, even to disapprove mildly, but the candid spectator will admit that their tricks inspire above all else a feeling of moral liberation. Jack's double life may be exposed, Algy's Bunbury may be deprived of his existence, but these deceptions serve their purpose, and part of us at least is glad.

Gwendolen and Cecily rely on beautiful untrue things as much as their suitors do, but instead of deceiving the world through imposture, they demand that the world accept the pleasing fantasies they choose to project onto it. The heroes adopt identities to suit the occasion; the heroines imagine identities to suit the persons with whom they choose to associate. Gwendolen explains her principles in love: "We live, as I hope you know, Mr Worthing, in an age of ideals. The fact is constantly mentioned in the more expensive monthly magazines, and has reached the provincial pulpits, I am told. And my ideal has always been to love someone of the name of Ernest. There is something in that name that inspires absolute confidence." She is very firm about this, and Cecily, whose words on the subject are almost identical, is nearly as firm. The comic parallel generates a certain irony against the girls; we are tempted to laugh at them for sharing a folly, yet we cannot help admiring the strength of their resolution, absurd though it is. Though idealism is burlesqued, we are made to admire the wit and courage required to impose a pattern on the world, even such a one as this.

The women in the play are generally stronger and more resourceful than the men. The latter are forced to prevaricate in a way that at times seems shuffling, even abject, whereas the former are always perfectly poised and move with imperturbable grace from one contradictory posture to another. I suspect that this has something to do with Wilde's own personality and personal history, but the pattern makes sense on its own terms. The play may be seen as a disquisition in favor of a set of attitudes more normally associated with women than with men. It commends the sort of character that accepts experience, with all its confusions, and accommodates itself through provisional opportunist adjustments—through style, in short. It pokes fun at hard and fast ideas about reality, at that aggressive kind of intelligence which seeks to control reality through theory. Rightly or wrongly, women are thought of as conforming more often to the subtle stereotype; men are thought of as conforming more often to the aggressive stereotype. Wilde was not simplistic about this. The embodiment of aggressive masculine intelligence in the play is Miss Prism, but that is part of the joke against her. The other women are naturally more at home in Wilde's world than the men.

Lady Bracknell, of course, is the character that most thoroughly exemplifies feminine strength. Delightful though she is, she is likely at first to baffle the audience's expectations because she is cast in the role of obstructionist to the lovers; in a conventional romantic comedy she would have to be defeated and humiliated. Yet that is not what happens to her, and it is difficult even to imagine it happening. The critics have recognized that she rises above this role; she has even been called a goddess. Satisfaction is what Lady Bracknell requires, not defeat, because, irrespective of her role, she is the character that embodies most forcibly Wilde's notions about the creative power of the imagination. Out of the nebulous material of society fashion, she wills into being a world of rock-hard solidity, obedient to her dispensation, before which all other worlds, real and imagined, fade into ghostly insubstantiality. The audience may laugh at the burlesque of a fashionable hostess, but there is reverence in the laughter. Her directives on the acceptable and the proper are not empirical observations on the state of fashion; they are the utterances of a lawgiver, endowed with all but divine afflatus. Her response to Jack's Belgrave Square address is typical:

> LADY BRACKNELL: The unfashionable side. However, that could easily be altered.
> JACK: Do you mean the fashion or the side, Lady Bracknell?
> LADY BRACKNELL: Both if necessary, I presume.

In contrast to the characters of farce who are imprisoned by manners, Lady Bracknell makes manners, and all the trivia of fashion, the building material of a world in which her will is law. She obtains freedom through manners, and she is powerful becauses she can impose her world on others.

Miss Prism and Dr. Chasuble are funny because they fail to impose their worlds on others, and in failing weakly parody the central characters. Their trouble is that they do not realize what they are doing and think that their rules and theories represent a real, substantial, unchanging world. Dr. Chasuble calls Miss Prism Egeria (an appellation much better suited to Lady Bracknell), but though she enunciates laws and definitions, they are tamely borrowed, not her own. Her paradoxes are amusing, not because they represent an attempt through wit to impose order on confusion, contradiction, and human folly, but because they indicate an unawareness of these things. Indeed, she does not realize that they are paradoxes. The audience laughs at her, not with her, when she describes her novel thus: "The good ended happily, and the bad unhappily. That is what Fiction means." Clearly she is a fit partner for Dr. Chasuble, who is thoroughly insensitive to the present moment (he is always misinterpreting the situation) and given to forcing an all-purpose moral onto any situation. His famous sermon is an example: "My sermon on the meaning of the manna in the wilderness can be adapted to almost any occasion, joyful, or, as in the present case, distressing. I have preached it at harvest celebrations, christenings, confirmations, on days of humiliation and festal days." Both Miss Prism's novel and Dr. Chasuble's sermon, it is clear, recommend an ordered picture of the world, which excludes the sense of absurdity behind order, central to Wilde's vision, a sense that *The Importance of Being Earnest,* in its entirety, practically demonstrates.

It is beyond the scope of this essay to fit the suggested interpretation of the play into the general scheme of Wilde's ideas, but it is not difficult to see how it may be reconciled with Wilde's views on art, individuality, morality, crime, politics, and so on. What I have tried to do is to provide an interpretation fitting in with notions concerning farce, the drama of the absurd, and existentialist theories of identity, all of which have been fashionable in recent years. This can certainly help us like and understand the play, but I do not wish it to be thought that I am suggesting it be admired because it is "relevant" (whatever that word might mean nowadays). It seems to me that it should be admired, not simply because it expresses a characteristically modern sensibility, nor even because it does so before its time, prophetically, but because it does so supremely well. It is possible to dislike the play, on grounds similar to those set out by Mary McCarthy, if only because it is possible to dislike the sort of sensibility it expresses. Its vehicle, the literary tradition to which I suggest the play belongs, is one that readily allows the writer to sink into self-indulgence. Some feel it permits little else nowadays. But I think that if we are prepared to accept the sensibility and the tradition as capable of producing excellence (if, in other words, we are prepared to adopt appropriate standards in judging the play), we are compelled to recognize the excellence of Wilde's play. To the contemplation of Nothingness, of the absurd, Wilde brings qualities of wit, intelligence, and (not least) appetite for life, rarely found so abundantly in such a context. *The Importance of Being Earnest* is a great farce because it transcends the normal limitations of the form. Wilde used the form to make a play that is sparkling, but profound as well.

The Providential Pun

Rodney Shewan

> *The hero of the future is he who shall bravely and gracefully subdue this Gorgon of fashion and convention.*
>
> "Art and the Handicraftsman"
>
> *I don't really know what a Gorgon is like, but I am quite sure that Lady Bracknell is one.*
>
> Jack to Algernon, *Earnest,* act 1

Wilde's last play, "a trivial comedy for serious people," is the dandy's holiday, a treat for "the few choice spirits," an idyllic trip to the utopian land of "doing as one likes" where only reason and external authority are denied entry. The text passed through various forms and was cut from four acts to three (robbing Wilde of his revenge on Du Maurier) but these vicissitudes strengthened it and it is rightly considered his tautest and most accomplished achievement. A summary and send-up of all his major themes, whether neo-Restoration, Romantic, or Victorian, and of practically all his critical or comic antitheses, it is the imaginative synthesis of its author's career and personality, and, paradoxically, the only work with which he succeeded completely in penetrating the fortress of established morality. For Mary McCarthy, indeed, it is the culmination of Wilde's usual propensity to make himself too much at home: "Where the usual work of art invites the spectator into its world, already furnished and habitable, Wilde's plays do just the opposite: the author invites himself and his fast opinions into the world of the spectator." No doubt Wilde would retort that, if the artist did not invite himself into the usual world, he would never be invited anywhere by anyone. Even so, Miss McCarthy's complaint

---

From *Oscar Wilde: Art and Egotism.* © 1977 by Rodney Shewan. Macmillan, 1977.

49

can hardly be justified by *Earnest,* a work which, whatever its debts to comic tradition or its feints towards social satire, creates and exhausts its own genre. Here, no one enters except by self-admission, for the play's burden is simply "Be thyself." Since this proposition had proved impossible in all other genres, Wilde posits absurdity as the norm in order to keep at bay those "other people" whose opinions are "vulgar" and "impossible."

Although the play contains elements of comic autobiography and parody confessional, it is primarily a highly original fusion of Wilde's idiosyncratic redemptive comedy and his basically anarchic assumptions. Algernon, the confirmed Bunburyist, and Jack, the reluctant guardian, are finally confronted with their alter egos only to see them dissolve hilariously into their actual selves. The author scours the realm of his "infernal Arcadia" like a benevolent maenad, dismembering his various literary aliases and tossing their limbs to anyone who can laugh. From this intoxicating, self-regenerating, self-fulfilling laughter only Lady Bracknell is excluded. Laughter in one who is "a monster without being a myth" would clearly be out of place. Those to whom the proper aim of life is to "gorgonise" the world with "a stony British stare" end up, Wilde says, by turning themselves into stone. For Lady Bracknell makes too many mistakes to be the bulky "goddess" of Mary McCarthy's vision. Once, perhaps, she might have filled the role of goddess—possibly of all-knowing Athena, "whose white and stainless bosom bears the sign Gorgonian," mistress and arbiter of the steep heights of London society. But no one can believe in a divinity who is forced to pay for information, obliged to travel by a luggage train, and who seems as much at the mercy of the deus ex machina as the merest mortal. Equally clearly, she makes too few mistakes to be really human. Pretending not to be a person, earnestly saving face, she alone grows no wiser and gets no fun.

The element of self-parody in *Earnest* has long been realized, although its extent was not fully known until the publication of a limited edition of Wilde's drafts, and, more recently, of the four-act version originally prepared for rehearsal. For once, external rather than internal pressures edited Wilde's autobiographical touches out of the published work. George Alexander wanted to put on a curtain-raiser, and so Wilde cut two characters— a dispensable rustic gardener and a shady solicitor, the latter being his revenge on Du Maurier. With the solicitor went the moist specific references to Wilde's own debts: the writ from the Savoy Hotel (Wilde's unpaid bill there prevented all possibility of flight before the trial in 1895), the huge supper bill at Willis's (where Wilde often fed Douglas, "Perrier-Jouet" being his favourite brand of champagne), and the account at a Bond Street jeweller

(Wilde reminded Douglas, in *De Profundis,* of the sleeve-links he had had made for him). The "private cigarette case" with its tell-tale inscription was multiplied at the trials, while the gold-tipped cigarettes despised by Algernon, now that they have become cheap, were always beyond the means of the brainless Lord Alfred of *A Woman of No Importance* except when he was in debt.

The earlier drafts also contain more explicit literary self-parody. Cecily twice refers to the doctrine of "The Decay of Lying" to justify her indulging in what Wilde had there termed "lying for some immediate personal advantage—lying with a moral purpose as it is usually called." She also quotes one of the "Phrases and Philosophies for the Use of the Young," given to the *Chameleon,* an Oxford undergraduate magazine, about the time that Wilde completed the play: "Believe me, Miss Prism, it is only the superficial qualities that last. Man's deeper nature is soon found out." Prism's response—"Cecily! I do not know where you get such ideas. They are certainly not to be found in any of the educational books that I have procured for you"—and Cecily's retort—"Are there ever any ideas in educational books, dear [Miss] Prism? I fear not. I get my ideas in the garden"—quantify not only the tutorial relationship between the women but also the studied precociousness of the whole work. "In examinations," Wilde had quipped, "the foolish ask questions that the wise cannot answer," and in *Earnest* life itself becomes a burlesque exam. Prism's confusion of a book with a baby (fatal in a governess), the Canon's ineptitude with metaphor (crucial in a cleric), and Jack's ridiculous viva voce at the hands of Lady Bracknell, the "really affectionate mother" who is actually his aunt, all tend to confirm that, if ever the older generation had the secret of life, they have long since lost it, and that it can only be regained by the "experimental" approach, a prime example of which is Bunburying. Even Gwendolen, who was brought up "to be short-sighted" and who attends the lectures of the University Extension scheme, undermines the idea of Higher Education for Women—or of formal education for anybody—by never coming away "without having been excessively admired."

The three-act version preserves a number of such echoes, and their diverse origins testify to the flexibility, or restlessness, of Wilde's mirror-gazing. Algy, the experienced Bunburyist stammering his passion to Cecily, quotes from Darlington's declaration to Lady Windermere. The scene is even written to sound like an actor "drying," while in Darlington's speech we can also detect the seed of Cecily's imaginary engagement: "I love you— love you as I have never loved any living thing. From the moment I met you I loved you, loved you blindly, adoringly, madly! You did not know it then—you know it now." What Algernon's speech does not owe to Darlington has been borrowed from the Basil of the first *Dorian Gray:* "I quite admit that I adored you madly, extravagantly, absurdly," he told Dorian; and the 1891 text continues, "you became to me the visible incarnation of that unseen ideal whose memory haunts us artists like an exquisite dream." But the parody runs deeper than dialogue. Convinced, perhaps, that its impossible relationships could be resolved only in farce, Wilde overhauls *A Woman of No Importance* to create a dramatic structure in which the parallels with Restoration comedy are finally explicit, and where the moral tolerance of redemptive comedy can be relaxed. The duties of the dandy-mediator are taken over by Providence, and Providence, here, is only another name for personality. To perfect this unlikely equation, Wilde plumps up Lady Caroline Pontefract to make Lady Bracknell; demotes Archdeacon Daubeny into Canon Chasuble; turns Gerald, the aristocrat's bastard, into a Justice of the Peace, giving him a pastoral maiden as ward, a profligate alter ego, and comically murky origins; turns Illingworth, his libertine father, into Algernon, his "wicked" younger brother; and shrinks Mrs Arbuthnot, his guilt-ridden mother, into Miss Prism, his ward's chaperone and tutor, the maiden lady whose youthful error with a baby is the crux of the plot. The false dénouement completes the dramatic prank: "Miss Prism, more is restored to you than this hand-bag. I was the baby you placed in it. . . . Unmarried! I do not deny that is a serious blow. But after all, who has the right to cast a stone against one who has suffered? Cannot repentance wipe out an act of folly? Why should there be one law for men, and another for women? Mother, I forgive you." Jan Gordon has argued that the search for historical, or family, origins is central to Victorian fiction, and has pointed out instances of the search in Wilde's tales. The theory might be extended to *Earnest,* for the sense of psychological disunity or incompleteness which gave rise to such a search is resolved in Wilde's last play with an originality that fully justifies his claim to have subjectified the drama to an unprecedented degree.

One further echo of *A Woman of No Importance* is relevant here. The dandy, Mrs Allonby, had married a pattern Victorian husband whose chin was "quite, quite square," and, finding herself "horribly deceived in Ernest," had projected a wholly different sort of Ideal Man. Wilde's last play reverses the situation. Both girls become engaged to an imaginary Ernest. "We live in an age of ideals," says Gwendolen, pompously, "and my ideal has always been to love someone of the name of Ernest." When Jack, whom she likes, discovers that he was christened Ernest after his soldierly father, she is satisfied. She lives and loves by appearances, and Jack, as Algernon says, is "the most earnest-looking person I ever saw in my life." For Jack, being "earnest" means simply being who he is: Ernest. Cecily, on the other hand, has become engaged in her private fictional world to Jack's "wicked younger brother" Ernest, so that her romance, too, parodies a Victorian fictional stereotype. When Algernon, wooing her as Ernest, is revealed to be Jack's real younger brother, even though not named Ernest, and shows, if not wickedness, at least a rampant propensity towards self-indulgence and a healthy disregard for all those virtues most often invoked by Miss Prism, Cecily also is satisfied. For her, the character of the "wicked younger brother," the character which stirred her imagination, is more important than his name. In this way, all four bring their ideal into working relationship with reality. Algernon and Jack find that they have been living out the essential truth unawares. Cecily and Gwendolen come to relish the approximate embodiment of their airy ideals. Discipline, idealism, convention, or mere habit may impose themselves on us and hinder our development; but our fantasies and self-projections, Wilde suggests, are every bit as much in earnest as our public gestures, poses, or undertakings. Imagination is the real symptom of a healthy life: "People never think of cultivating a young girl's imagination. It is the great defect of modern education."

Thus Cecily's references to "The Decay of Lying" were not without their thematic point. The "telling of beautiful untrue things" determines the action of the play. The higher reality is reached here through falsehood, "lying." If the artist's labours can be seen as a "gallant attempt to teach Nature her proper place," the creative individual is no less gallant in trying to teach Society hers. Perhaps that is why Shaw thought *Earnest* a step backwards—could not believe, in fact, that Wilde had not written it earlier and somehow kept it unsold. For the play shows that while Society, like Nature, "has good intentions," she can "seldom carry them out." Recognising in instincts her own murky past and in imagination her own embarrassing and voluble bastard, Society plays the role of "a really affectionate mother" and tries to overlay them. But in farce, the latter-day Feast of Fools, they can spring free. Farce places fate in the artist's hand, and with this tool he shapes Dionysiac revel into Apollonian perfection of form. It may be a coincidence that the contemporary slang term used in Wilde's circle to refer to homosexual revels was "wearing vine-leaves in the hair." (Beardsley represented Wilde, in the frontispiece to John Davidson's *Plays*, as a placid Dionysus who seems to have his feet tied together.) It is clear enough that here—"at last!"—the individual's conscious and unconscious motives, idea and instinct, work in secret coalition to produce that ever-

alluring combination of "personality" and "perfection": "being earnest."
For the artist, Wilde had written earlier, "there is no escape from the
bondage of the earth: there is not even the desire of escape." The same
might be said of the artist and the bondage of the self. Even for the nonartist,
escape from the self may finally prove impossible, whether one tries to
identify one's self with the authority of convention or with those anarchic
spirits who strike out against it. "Disobedience," however, "is the first step
in the growth of a man or a nation," and disobedience, irresponsibility,
and contradiction lead here to universal harmony and happiness. The only
character who gains nothing is the one who thinks only of the rules—Lady
Bracknell, Society herself.

Farce is thus the ultimate refinement of pastoral, the new idyll of self,
the egotist's Nirvana. The "child-philosopher" of Wilde's first set of fairy
tales is replaced by its adult equivalent, the fearless ingénue with "the
fascinating tyranny of youth." In that garden where romance buds and
learning withers, and where she had first rejected fact for fiction, Cecily
falls from art into life; tames the rake; unites town and country, "science"
and "sentiment"; reconciles the demure spinster of Hebraism with the reluctant bachelor of Hellenism; "explodes" vice and virtue as if they were
no more than the dull people's Bunburys: "I hope you have not been leading
a double life, pretending to be wicked and being really good all the time;
that would be hypocrisy." She knows by instinct that, just as "seriousness
of manner is the disguise of the fool," so "folly in its exquisite modes of
triviality and indifference and lack of care is the robe of the wise." She also
senses, despite her distaste for German and political economy, that Lady
Bracknell's reactionary notion of education—"Ignorance is like a delicate,
exotic fruit: touch it, and the bloom is gone"—is all wrong, not for social
but for personal reasons. Fruits, even delicate exotic fruits, were not made
just to be looked at, nor are young girls necessarily "green." Formal education may often amount to no more than gazing at the ignorance of
others, but there is no more delicious prospect than biting into one's own
ignorance. In this, Algernon is at one with her, both of them being as far
ahead of Jack and Gwendolen as those two are ahead of the older generation.
Lady Bracknell is alarmed to see Jack "displaying signs of triviality" (he is
kissing Gwendolen), but he knows at last "the vital Importance of Being
Earnest." Chasuble is horrified at the "disgraceful luxury of the age" as
exemplified by Ernest's colossal supper bill: "We are far from Wordsworth's
plain living and high thinking," he sighs. But Algernon knows how far
behind the times the Canon is in his estimate of the progress of sin. When
he asks Cecily whether she will make it her "mission" to "reform" him,

a suggestion to which she does not take kindly, she questions whether he ever was good. "Oh," he replies, "everyone is good until they learn to talk." It is the social conversationalist's account of the fortunate fall. If we were not bad, we would never have the chance of talking to Cousin Cecily, and it is this chance which enables Algernon to talk himself into harmony with a newly completed family, newly completed feelings, and a new awareness of himself. Lastly, Lady Bracknell objects that "in families of high social position strange coincidences are not supposed to occur," but Cecily, the orphan, wins hands down. Society discovers that she has a large sum in the Funds; but she also possesses "those really solid qualities" that "last and improve with time." She knows that the basis of family, as of personal, life—always in its ideal manifestation—is knowing, showing, and living who you really are.

The Triumph of the Pleasure Principle

Katharine Worth

The Importance of Being Earnest is Wilde's funniest play and it is also the most poignant, if we have in mind—as how can we not?—the disaster that struck its author only a few weeks after its glittering first night when Queensberry instigated the process that led to Reading Gaol. It was just the terrible peripeteia he had imagined for Robert Chiltern: one moment the "splendid position," the next, public humiliation and the odious gloating of hypocrites. The fall was symbolically encapsulated in the fate of the posters advertising the new play and also *An Ideal Husband* which was still running at the Haymarket. A splendid position indeed, to have two plays enjoying huge success side by side in London's most fashionable theatres. Yet is was wiped out overnight, when Wilde's name was obliterated from the posters, by George Alexander at the St James's, and Lewis Waller at the Haymarket. It is something to set against the weakness of the two actors, who owed so much to Wilde, the courage of Charles Wyndham who refused to receive *An Ideal Husband* at his theatre, the Criterion (where it had been scheduled to move), unless Wilde's name were restored to the bills. And this was done.

In *The Importance of Being Earnest* the pleasure principle at last enjoys complete triumph. Some critics disapprove of this, notably Mary McCarthy who censures the dandies' determination to live a life of pleasure as "selfishness." Perhaps it is, but we are not being required to examine their moral behaviour in humane Chekhovian terms. This is a philosophical farce, an existential farce, to use the modern term which modern criticism is begin-

From *Oscar Wilde*. © 1983 by Katharine Worth. Macmillan, 1983.

ning to see as appropriate for this witty exploration of identities. "Pleasure," a word which recurs much, is a shorthand for the idea Wilde expounded in "The Soul of Man under Socialism":

> Pleasure is Nature's test, her sign of approval. When man is happy, he is in harmony with himself and his environment. The new Individualism, for whose service Socialism, whether it wills it or not, is working, will be perfect harmony.

Only in Utopia can this harmony be achieved; in theatrical terms that meant farce, the form that refused the agonies of melodrama. Wilde had observed that farce and burlesque offered the artist in England more freedom than the "higher" forms of drama. He was following Nietzsche, who had said much the same thing a decade or so earlier. In this extravagant genre, which no one took seriously, the dionysiac spirit could be fully released, to overturn respectable reality, and through paradox, fantasy and contradiction establish a logic of its own, defying the censorious superego. As Wilde put it in an interview given before the first production, the philosophy of his piece is that "we should treat all the trivial things of life very seriously and all the serious things of life with sincere and studied triviality." It is a play of mirror images in which ordinary, everyday life can still be glimpsed through the comic distortions imposed upon it. Everything is double, from the double life of Algernon and Jack to the sets of doubles at the end, when the girls form themselves into opposition to the male image which has so conspicuously failed to be "Ernest."

In this play more than in any of the others it is vital for the actors to seem unaware of the absurdity of what they do and say. In the first production Irene Vanbrugh, playing Gwendolen, was paralysed with terror at being unable to find the right style; someone advised her to "think" the lines before speaking them, and she felt she then became more natural. However, according to Shaw, the actors in the first production were insufferably affected: Cecily had too much conscious charm, the older ladies too much low comedy; even George Alexander, whose grave, refined manner as Jack made suitable contrast with Algernon's easygoing style, ruined the third act by bustling through at such a rate that he quite lost the "subdued earnestness" which Shaw felt should characterise the role. (Wilde had doubted his suitability for the part.) A few years later (in the 1902 revival at the St James's) Max Beerbohm found the actors making the same mistakes. Only Lilian Braithwaite "in seeming to take her part quite seriously, showed that she had realised the full extent of its fun." George Alexander was still bustling—at breakneck speed—and the part of Chasuble was played "as though it were a minutely realistic character study of the typical country clergyman."

"Everything matters in art except the subject," said Wilde. In *The Importance of Being Earnest* the subject certainly cannot be distinguished from the style, yet the fact that the play succeeded (as it did on both the occasions quoted) even when the actors were playing it wrongly shows what a steely construction it has. It must have given Wilde the craftsman much pleasure to take the familiar melodrama mechanism (mistaken identities, incriminating inscriptions, secrets of the past) and exploit its inherent absurdity instead of trying to restrain it. The closeness of farce to melodrama is one of his strong cards, in fact, allowing all kinds of oblique references to the oppressive moral laws which had malign consequences in the earlier plays—and, as Wilde thought, in English society. As well as being an existential farce, *The Importance of Being Earnest* is his supreme demolition of late nineteenth-century social and moral attitudes, the triumphal conclusion to his career as revolutionary moralist.

Wilde has sometimes been seen as an overtolerant, even careless craftsman, only too ready to accept textual alterations called for by his actor-managers. *The Importance of Being Earnest* has been cited as an illustration: it was originally in the more usual four-act form, but when Alexander asked him to shorten it (almost unbelievably, to make room for a curtain raiser) Wilde obliged him to the extent of dropping the third act. As Lady Bracknell might have said, to lose a scene or two might be regarded as a misfortune, to lose a whole act seems like carelessness. However, if we study the four-act draft, we can see how far from carelessly Wilde made his revisions and indeed how much the play is improved by rigorous cutting which gives it a more spare and modern look. Farce should have the speed of a pistol shot, said Wilde, and speed is, indeed, a distinctive and curious feature of *The Importance of Being Earnest;* curious, because it coexists with extreme slowness and stateliness in the dialogue. No one is ever so agitated that he cannot take time to round a sentence, find the right metaphor—or finish off the last muffin. Yet all the time sensational changes are occurring at the speed of light. Proposals of marriage are found to have been received even before they were uttered, relations lost and found before one can say "handbag." Time, like everything else, goes double and through the "gaps" Wilde insinuates the notion that the action is really all happening somewhere else, in the mental dimension where ruling fantasies are conceived, which is not to say of course that there is no connection with reality: "Life imitates Art far more than Art imitates life." The outlines of reality are easily discernible; Lane offering deadpan excuses for the absence of cucumber sandwiches, Dr

Chasuble fitting in the absurd christening to his perfectly normal programme: "In fact I have two similar ceremonies to perform at that time. A case of twins that occurred recently in one of the outlying cottages on your own estate. Poor Jenkins the carter, a most hard-working man." What is wrong with this society, so the farce implies, is its fatal inability to distinguish between the trivial and the serious. Sense and nonsense, reason and fantasy, facts and truth, are juggled with, forcing new perspectives, offering release from the cramp of habit and logic:

> ALGERNON: Please don't touch the cucumber sandwiches. They
>   are ordered specially for Aunt Augusta. (*Takes one and*
>   *eats it.*)
> JACK: Well, you have been eating them all the time.
> ALGERNON: That is quite a different matter. She is my aunt.

How can one challenge the impeccable logic of this? Only by lapsing into earnestness, which the play is set up expressly to forbid. Shaw's complaint that the farce was never lifted onto a higher lane was an extraordinary failure of judgment for him. How good-humoured of Wilde to say only "I am disappointed in you."

It is an urbane Utopia we see when the curtain goes up on the first act. Algernon's rooms in Half Moon Street (a more relaxed environment than the grand locales of earlier plays) are "luxuriously and artistically furnished"; music is heard from the off-stage piano (perhaps a dubious pleasure, as Algernon saves his science for life and relies on sentiment in his piano playing). The elegant sallies between Algernon and his "ideal butler," Lane, are another feature of Wilde's Utopia; servants are more than equal to masters. With the entrance of Jack, the "pleasure" motif rings out loud and clear:

> ALGERNON: How are you, my dear Ernest? What brings you
>   up to town?
> JACK: Oh pleasure, pleasure! What else should bring one
>   anywhere.

Tom Stoppard lifted this debonair entrance to serve as a "time stop" in *Travesties,* a sticking place in the mind to which the action obsessively returns. He assigns Jack's lines to Tristan Tzara, the Dadaist, making a connection between the pleasure philosophy, revolution and nihilism. Jack and Algernon are not exactly revolutionaries, but they do bring into the play from time to time a rather modern emphasis on the idea of nothingness, as when they discuss ways they might spend the evening:

ALGERNON: What shall we do after dinner? Go to a theatre?
JACK: Oh no! I loathe listening.
ALGERNON: Well, let us go to the Club?
JACK: Oh no! I hate talking.
ALGERNON: Well, we might trot round to the Empire at ten?
JACK: Oh no! I can't bear looking at things. It is so silly.
ALGERNON: Well, what shall we do?
JACK: Nothing!

The malaise is kept at bay most of the time by the complications of the double life. Wilde amusingly recalls the impassioned detective sequences of *An Ideal Husband* in the inquisition conducted by Algernon into Jack's secrets. A precious mislaid object, the inscribed cigarette case, provides a crucial clue (parallelling the bracelet/brooch of the other play); Algernon presses his questions as unremittingly as Lady Chiltern ("But why does she call you little Cecily, if she is your aunt and lives at Tunbridge Wells?") and like Robert Chiltern, Jack fights off discovery with inventive lies. "Earnest" was the word for the Chiltern double life and "Earnest" is the word for Jack's too, in the double sense perceived by Algernon the moment Jack reveals his "real" name:

ALGERNON: Besides, your name isn't Jack at all; it is Ernest.
JACK: It isn't Ernest; it's Jack.
ALGERNON: You have always told me it was Ernest. I have
    introduced you to everyone as Ernest. You answer to the
    name of Ernest. You look as if your name is Ernest. You
    are the most earnest-looking person I ever saw in my life.

The brilliant pun is the cornerstone of a structure dedicated to dualities of all kinds. Jack is "Ernest in town and Jack in the country": he becomes "Ernest" in fact when he wants to escape from being "earnest"; the pun perfectly encapsulates the split in the personality. Neatness, taken to the point of surrealist absurdity, makes the same sort of suggestion throughout. Algernon's situation is a mirror image of Jack's. When he sums up the situation, he falls into a rhythm which is the quintessential rhythm of the play; a balancing of opposites, the "masks," which as the play goes on are to be juggled with increasingly manic ingenuity:

You have invented a very useful younger brother called Ernest
in order that you may be able to come up to town as often as
you like. I have invented an invaluable permanent invalid called

Bunbury, in order that I may be able to go down into the country whenever I choose.

Critics in Wilde's time did not grasp the subtlety of the structure. Even Max Beerbohm, an admirer, thought the play triumphed despite its farcical "scheme" which he summarised as: "the story of a young man coming up to London 'on the spree,' and of another young man going down conversely to the country, and of the complications that ensue." This comes nowhere near expressing the mysterious sense of what "town" and "country" represent for Jack and Algernon. "On the spree" is a phrase for the French *boulevard* farce and its "naughty" behaviour, which English audiences could enjoy in suitably watered down adaptations, with a feeling of moral superiority. Wilde slyly draws attention to this characteristic hypocrisy when Algernon gives Jack some very French advice:

> ALGERNON: A man who marries without knowing Bunbury
> has a very tedious time of it.
> JACK: That is nonsense. If I marry a charming girl like
> Gwendolen, and she is the only girl I ever saw in my life
> that I would marry, I certainly won't want to know
> Bunbury.
> ALGERNON: Then your wife will. You don't seem to realise,
> that in married life three is company and two is none.
> JACK (*sententiously*): That, my dear young friend, is the theory
> that the corrupt French Drama has been propounding for
> the last fifty years.
> ALGERNON: Yes; and that the happy English home has proved
> in half the time.

There is little sense in the play of orgiastic goings on. "Eating" is the chief symbol of sensual activity. The dandies' will to eat is part of the larger will which drives them and the girls (and indeed everyone in the play). Shaw might have called it the Life Force. Wilde uses a favourite metaphor: health. As Jack explains to Algernon, he needs Ernest because as Uncle Jack he is expected to maintain a high moral tone, and a high moral tone can hardly be said to conduce to one's health or happiness. We might wonder why the insouciant Algernon needs an escape route. But we find out when Lady Bracknell appears on the scene, ringing the bell in "Wagnerian manner" and greeting her nephew in a most remarkable variant of common usage: "I hope you are behaving very well?" He fights back with "I'm feeling very well, Aunt Augusta," only to be overriden with magisterial finality:

"That is not quite the same thing. In fact the two rarely go together." Judi Dench's unusually youthful Lady Bracknell in the National Theatre's 1982 production clearly had a somewhat overfond interest in her elegant nephew, an unexpected slant which increased the psychological interest (Peter Hall, directing, saw the play as being "about love and about reality").

Lady Bracknell herself is dedicated to health; a supreme irony. As she tells Algernon when he produces Bunbury's illness yet again, as an excuse for avoiding her dinner party:

> I think it is high time that Mr Bunbury made up his mind
> whether he was going to live or to die. This shilly-shallying
> with the question is absurd. Nor do I in any way approve of
> the modern sympathy with invalids. I consider it morbid. Illness
> of any kind is hardly a thing to be encouraged in others. Health
> is the primary duty of life.

We can well see why Lord Bracknell had to become an invalid: she has taken all the health for herself. It is a measure of Wilde's ability to stand back from his own passionately held beliefs that the most completely realised personality in the play should be such a monster; as Jack says, "a monster without being a myth, which is rather unfair."

There is no doubt in this play that "women rule society." Lady Bracknell has a more central position in the dramatic action than the dowagers of earlier plays. The marriages are in her control, and it is she who (unwittingly) holds the key to Jack's identity. She comes on with Gwendolen in tow, in the manner of the Duchess of Berwick and Lady Agatha, and though Gwendolen is no Agatha, she is just as much in thrall to her mother when husbands are in question. On one of its levels the farce is certainly conducting the old campaign against the tyrannies that afflict women. There is an extra layer of irony indeed; we see how the system will perpetuate itself as the victims prepare to become tyrants in their turn, for Gwendolen is clearly her mother's daughter. It is not just a joke when Jack anxiously enquires: "You don't think there is any chance of Gwendolen becoming like her mother in about a hundred and fifty years, do you, Algy?" The proposal scene certainly gives him warning, with its focus on Gwendolen's will and the intensity of the inner life which surfaces (in appropriately "absurd" form) in her curious obsession:

> My ideal has always been to love someone of the name of Ernest.
> There is something in that name that inspires absolute confi-
> dence. The moment Algernon first mentioned to me that he had
> a friend called Ernest, I knew I was destined to love you.

There is obviously a dig here at the troublesome idealists of earlier plays: the whole ideal-oriented ethos is reduced to absurdity. It is a philosophical as well as a social joke, however. Could she not love him if he had some other name? "Ah!" says Gwendolen, "that is clearly a metaphysical speculation, and like most metaphysical speculations has very little reference at all to the actual facts of real life as we know them." She says it "glibly"; that is Wilde's joke, for though Gwendolen may be intellectually shallow, her devotion to her "ideal" reflects concepts Wilde took very seriously. Gwendolen is making the sacred effort to "realise one's own personality on some imaginative plane out of reach of the trammelling accidents and limitations of real life." When Jack calls her "perfect" she resists the term: "It would leave no room for developments, and I intend to develop in many directions."

The "limitations of real life" are soon imposed on the idyll when Lady Bracknell sweeps in, to surprise Jack on his knees: "Rise, sir, from this semi-recumbent posture. It is most indecorous." Her marriage questionnaire carries, in its absurd way, the whole weight of the commercially-minded society she epitomises:

> LADY BRACKNELL: What is your income?
>
> JACK: Between seven and eight thousand a year.
>
> LADY BRACKNELL (*makes a note in her book*): In land, or in investments?
>
> JACK: In investments, chiefly.
>
> LADY BRACKNELL: That is satisfactory. What between the duties expected of one during one's lifetime, and the duties exacted from one after one's death, land has ceased to be either a profit or a pleasure. It gives one position, and prevents one from keeping it up. That's all that can be said about land.

Anyone who can talk as well as this is bound to charm—still she cannot be thought totally charming. Real life is hovering there in the background, making us feel just a little mean at laughing when she holds forth on the nature of society from the height of her conservative hauteur. Her power is political as well as social; Wilde's point is that the two are one. Liberal Unionists are acceptable, she concedes, when Jack admits to being one: "they count as Tories. They dine with us. Or come in the evenings, at any rate." The fine shades of her condescension are droll, but a telling reminder of a real-life Byzantine grading system which ensures that politics are controlled by the right people.

It does not really matter what Jack admits to in the way of taste: there is no way of kowtowing to Lady Bracknell, for, as Mary McCarthy says, she has the unpredictability of a thorough grande dame. Jack is no doubt taken aback, as we are, by the remarkable triviality of her first question—"Do you smoke?"—and no doubt equally surprised by her response to his admission that he does:

> I am glad to hear it. A man should always have an occupation of some kind. There are far too many idle men in London as it is.

It makes him understandably wary when she declares that "a man who desires to get married should know either everything or nothing," and asks "which" he knows. It is only "after some hesitation" that he commits himself: "I know nothing, Lady Bracknell." A fitting remark for an existential hero. She, of course, takes it in a social sense, as she does everything, and approves; a rich irony, for Jack's devotion to "nothing" goes along with his mercurial changeability, something she would deeply disapprove of. "Knowing nothing" for her means "ignorance," a very desirable quality in the lower classes:

> The whole theory of modern education is radically unsound. Fortunately in England, at any rate, education produces no effect whatsoever. If it did, it would prove a serious danger to the upper classes, and probably lead to acts of violence in Grosvenor Square.

Great fun, in the context, yet are we meant to quite shut out reverberations from history—the Nihilists, the Irish, all the social ferment which troubled Wilde's conscience and is reflected in his other plays? It seems not, for the revolution theme comes up again in an explicit historical reference when Jack reveals the peculiar circumstances of his birth. Even Lady Bracknell cannot assimilate that anarchical phenomenon:

> I don't actually know who I am by birth. I was . . . well, I was found. . . . In a hand-bag—a somewhat large, black, leather hand-bag, with handles to it.

All her worst nightmares crowd—majestically—into the scene:

> To be born, or at any rate bred, in a hand-bag, whether it had handles or not, seems to me to display a contempt for the ordinary decencies of family life that reminds one of the worst

> excesses of the French Revolution. And I presume you know
> what that unfortunate movement led to?

This is no casual reference. The French Revolution figures in "The Soul of
Man under Socialism" as illustration of the inevitability of change: "The
systems that fail are those that rely on the permanency of human nature,
and not on its growth and development. The error of Louis XIV was that
he thought that human nature would always be the same. The result of his
error was the French Revolution. It was an admirable result." By analogy,
Lady Bracknell is necessary to the process she is resisting; Wilde provides
us with a moral justification for the fact that we cannot help liking the
monster!

There is also a little germ of existential anxiety in the great joke: "being"
in an empty handbag; being in a void. Like a Vladimir or a Winnie in
Beckett's empty spaces, Jack has to construct himself from virtually nothing. That is more or less what Lady Bracknell advises him to do before
she departs in high dudgeon at the idea of Gwendolen being asked to "marry
into a cloak-room, and form an alliance with a parcel." "I would strongly
advise you, Mr Worthing," she says, "to try and acquire some relations as
soon as possible." Ridiculous, yet it has already happened. Younger brother
Ernest is soon to acquire extraordinary reality. Jack's fertile imagination
rises to these challenges. "Gwendolen, I must get christened at once," was
his immediate reaction to the revelation that she could only love a man
called Ernest.

At the fall of the curtain on the first act the metaphysical dimension is
thickening. Jack is in a tortuous relationship with the mythic self which he
needs both to destroy ("I am going to kill my brother") and at the same
time possess more completely (by having himself christened, a comical
psychic ordeal). And Algernon, with the address of "excessively pretty
Cecily" surreptitiously registered on his shirt-cuff, is gleefully preparing
to get into his Bunbury clothes and take over the adaptable "Ernest" identity
for himself. The juggling with personae is becoming more and more "absurd" in the modern sense.

The second act opens in a garden, a utopian setting such as Wilde had
never quite allowed himself in earlier plays where the furthest we got into
nature was a lawn under a terrace (though one critic draws attention to
garden imagery in the dialogue of *A Woman of No Importance*). This is not
very wild nature, of course: still, there is emphasis on luxuriance (an old-
fashioned abundance of roses) and various hints that this is the scene where
growth and change are to be achieved. The "blue glass" stage floor and

cut-out garden accessories in Peter Hall's 1982 production struck the right note of artfully stylised simplicity. In the four-act version a gardener appeared, an unexpected addition to the usual cast of butlers and valets. Here Cecily (significantly seen at the back of the stage, deep in the garden) is doing the gardener's work, a fact Miss Prism observes with distaste:

> MISS PRISM (*calling*): Cecily, Cecily! Surely such a utilitarian occupation as the watering of flowers is rather Moulton's duty than yours? Especially at a moment when intellectual pleasures await you. Your German grammar is on the table. Pray open it at page fifteen. We will repeat yesterday's lesson.
>
> CECILY (*coming over very slowly*): But I don't like German. It isn't at all a becoming language. I know perfectly well that I look quite plain after my German lesson.

The reference to German as the bone of contention is no accident. Like the "pessimist" joke at the close of act 1 (Algernon accuses Lane of being a pessimist and is told "I always endeavour to give satisfaction, sir"), it is one of those oblique allusions to German philosophy which slyly suggest that the characters are enacting a Schopenhauer style struggle to realise the "will" and engage with the concept of "nothing." Jack always lays particular stress on the importance of Cecily's German when he goes off to town (to become his alter ego). So Miss Prism observes, while Cecily notes the strain involved: "Dear Uncle Jack is so very serious! Sometimes he is so serious that I think he cannot be quite well." She draws attention to the existential confusion which surely overtakes the audience by now. Who really is Jack/Ernest? Is he acting when he is serious Uncle Jack and is Ernest his true identity (as Gwendolen asserts)? Or is he really Jack struggling to manage the wicked brother, Ernest? He is often half way between the two, as the fluctuations in his style indicate. The man who entered the play on so airy a note ("Oh, pleasure, pleasure!") can talk very sententiously, and look the part too, as Algernon had observed.

Cecily has no such complications. Yet she is also in her way an existentialist, using her diary as the young men use Ernest to act out her "will." Wilde strikes very modern notes in the discussion sparked off by the diary about the difficulty of distinguishing between memory and fiction, both seen here as part of the self-creating process:

> CECILY: I keep a diary in order to enter the wonderful secrets of my life. If I didn't write them down, I should probably forget all about them.

> MISS PRISM: Memory, my dear Cecily, is the diary that we all
> carry about with us.
> CECILY: Yes, but it usually chronicles the things that have
> never happened, and couldn't possibly have happened. I
> believe that Memory is responsible for nearly all the
> three-volume novels that Mudie sends us.

Miss Prism's confession that she once wrote a three-volume novel (leading to her memorable definition: "The good ended happily, and the bad unhappily. That is what Fiction means") contributes to the Beckettian shades in the comedy. But she, like her other half, Canon Chasuble, is really essence of nineteenth century. Through their delicious absurdities we discern, like shadows, characteristics that had to be taken more grimly in earlier plays: pomposity, self-importance, cruelty even (Miss Prism is much given to pronouncing "As a man sows, so also shall he reap"). But rigid morality loses its power when the absurdly serious pair represent it. They have a foot in the utopian world.

Miss Prism too pursues a dream: "You are too much alone, dear Dr Chasuble. You should get married. A misanthrope I can understand—a womanthrope, never!" His scholarly shudder at the "neologistic" phrase reminds us, like his reference to Egeria which Miss Prism fails to understand ("My name is Laetitia, Doctor"), that there is a social gulf between them. She is hardly a highly-educated governess; we learn later that she started life as a nursemaid. Wilde is extending the satire on Victorian moral attitudes to take in the middle to lower classes, an interesting development which makes one more than ever sad at what may have been lost when catastrophe brought his playwriting to an end.

Cecily soon clears the stage for her own freedom. In her manipulation of the wobbling celibates ("it would do her so much good to have a short stroll with you in the park, Dr Chasuble"), she displays the masterfulness which makes her, like Gwendolen, more than a match for the men. Like a modern girl, she cuts Algernon down to size when he makes his appearance as Ernest on a somewhat arch note:

> ALGERNON: You are my little cousin, Cecily, I'm sure.
> CECILY: You are under some strange mistake. I am not little.
> In fact, I believe I am more than usually tall for my age.

Algernon, says the stage direction, is "rather taken aback." Well he might be: it is the end of his Bunburying days when Cecily takes charge, leading him into the house to start the process of "reforming" him.

It is an exquisite stroke of comic timing that at the very moment when brother Ernest has materialised for the first time, Jack should enter, in mourning for his death in Paris of a chill. Pictures of George Alexander in the part show him the very spirit of lugubriousness, in funereal black, with the "crepe hatband and black gloves" which Dr Chasuble calls his "garb of woe." It is a great visual joke, demonstrating, as C. E. Montague said, the scenic imagination which distinguishes playwrights from other writers: "To an audience, knowing what it knows, the mere first sight of those black clothes is convulsingly funny; it is a visible stroke of humour, a witticism not heard but seen." Wilde did not make much of the stage directions for *The Importance of Being Earnest*: they are less detailed than in earlier plays. When preparing proofs for publication in 1899, he remarked to Robert Ross that he did not much like giving physical details "about the bodies whose souls, or minds, or passions, I deal with. I build up so much out of *words* that the colour of people's hair seems unimportant." Yet Montague was right to stress the value of the scenic element. We do not need to know the colour of the characters' hair—what colour would Ernest's be?—but, as in all the plays, a delicate visual symbolism operates in *The Importance of Being Earnest*, crystallising underlying meanings. The spectacle of the "man in black" making those absurd arrangements to be christened ("Ah, that reminds me, you mentioned christenings, I think, Dr Chasuble?") is surely, for us now, an existential joke.

Of course none of this shows to the stage audience. Jack's rather disturbing fluidity of character is highlighted by the rigidity of Miss Prism and Canon Chasuble: they move on the narrowest of lines and appeal to our sense of humour by having none themselves. It is one of Wilde's most dionysiac moments of glee when Jack, acting solemnity, draws forth the real solemnity of the celibate pair:

CHASUBLE: Was the cause of death mentioned?
JACK: A severe chill, it seems.
MISS PRISM: As a man sows, so shall he reap.
CHASUBLE (*raising his hand*): Charity, dear Miss Prism, charity! None of us are perfect. I myself am peculiarly susceptible to draughts. Will the interment take place here?
JACK: No. He seems to have expressed a desire to be buried in Paris.
CHASUBLE: In Paris! (*shakes his head*) I fear that hardly points to any very serious state of mind at the last.

This is the sort of caricature which is more lifelike than life itself. The consistent pair are in their way an anchor to a solid world where we expect people to be much the same from one day to another. In the other dimension, where there seems no limit to the characters' ability to change themselves, the action is becoming manic:

> My brother is in the dining-room? I don't know what it all means. I think it is perfectly absurd.

It is "absurd" in Pinteresque vein when Jack, in mourning for Ernest, is impudently advised to "change":

> Why on earth don't you go up and change? It is perfectly childish to be in deep mourning for a man who is actually staying for a whole week with you in your house as a guest. I call it grotesque.

The alter ego is out of hand. Even the imperturbable Algernon is taken aback, in his second scene with Cecily, to realise how firmly she has defined his role in her "girlish dream." It was "on the 14th of February last that worn out by your entire ignorance of my existence, I determined to end the matter one way or the other, and after a long struggle with myself I accepted you under this dear old tree here." A very determined piece of dreaming, this,—a comical version of Schopenhauer's "world as idea"— held together, like Gwendolen's scenario, by the "ideal" Ernest.

Repetition and increasingly heavy stylisation from now on build up the impression that some psychic process is being acted out—in the absurd form appropriate to events in the unconscious. Algernon and Cecily must go through the same performance as Jack and Gwendolen; he must react in the same way as Jack to the realisation that "Ernest" is no longer a voluntary role by rushing off to be christened. And Gwendolen must appear, for a quarrel scene with Cecily which is in a way closer to the norm of nineteenth century comedy (Gilbert's *Engaged* was mentioned by contemporary critics), but acquires strangeness from the dreamlike gap Wilde contrives between the solid, decorous surface (Merriman totally absorbed in supervising the tea-table rites) and the increasingly uninhibited argument about someone who doesn't exist. As the lines become ever more crossed— "Oh, but it is not Mr Ernest Worthing who is my guardian. It is his brother—his elder brother"—the audience has almost certainly lost its own grip on who is who, a confusion Wilde surely intends.

He evidently intends also the exaggerated stylisation which begins to push the farce away from even minimal realism when Jack and Algernon are brought face to face with Gwendolen and Cecily. Like automata, the girls ask the same questions and use the same movements, each in turn demanding of "her" Ernest, "May I ask if you are engaged to be married to this young lady?" and on receiving the desired assurance, proceeding to prick the bubble of the other's dream with a mannered precision which has drawn from modern critics terms like "courtship dance" to describe the manoeuvrings of the quartet:

> The gentleman whose arm is at present round your waist is my guardian, Mr John Worthing.

> The gentleman who is now embracing you is my cousin, Mr Algernon Moncrieff.

The breaking up and reforming of pairs, the neat oppositions, the stilted repetitions, the speaking for each other (Gwendolen takes over Cecily's unformed question, "Where is your brother Ernest?"); all create a curious impression, of personality flowing unstoppably between two poles. Everything surprises us by being its own opposite ("A truth in Art is that whose contradictory is also true"). Things taken with deadly seriousness in the "modern life" plays are stood on their head, as in Jack's parodic confession:

> Gwendolen—Cecily—it is very painful for me to be forced to speak the truth. It is the first time in my life I have ever been reduced to such a painful position, and I am really quite inexperienced in doing anything of the kind. However I will tell you quite frankly that I have no brother Ernest.

A subtle joke; for by the end we know that his brilliant invention was the truth; it was the facts that were untrustworthy ("Life imitates art far more than art imitates life").

Before we arrive at that revelation, the doubles have to reorganise themselves. The female pair retire into the house "with scornful looks" and the male pair are left to pick up the pieces of the shattered personality. Time is going round in circles; we are almost back in the first act with the cucumber sandwiches when Algernon settles down to the muffins and Jack reproaches him: "How you can sit there calmly eating muffins, when we are in this horrible trouble, I can't make out. You seem to me to be perfectly heartless." Never for him, it seems, the intellectual aplomb which allows Algernon to short-circuit "absurd" anxieties with absurd and unanswerable logic: "Well, I can't eat muffins in an agitated manner. The butter would probably get on my cuffs."

In the final act we move back into the house; the garden idyll (the "beautiful" act, Wilde called it) is over, the "truth" is out and time is flowing back towards daylight. Gwendolen and Cecily are seen looking out of the windows at the young men, as if no time at all has elapsed, or just enough for them to say, in the past tense, "they have been eating muffins." Stylisation reaches its peak when the young men join them and both pairs address each other in choral unison, Gwendolen beating time "with up-lifted finger." In an early draft, this went on longer and lines were split between characters, as Russell Jackson says, accentuating the effect of a duet. It is an altogether musical scene: the men come on whistling "some dreadful popular air from a British opera" (not identified, but could Wilde wickedly have intended *Patience*?). In earlier drafts the stylisation was even more extreme and balletic. Jack and Algernon were to "move together like Siamese twins in every movement" when they make their announcement that they are to be christened:

> First to front of sofa, then fold hands together, then raise eyes
> to ceiling, then sit on sofa, unfold hands, lean back, tilting up
> legs with both feet off the ground, then twitch trousers above
> knee à la dude.

It is almost surrealist farce now; Jarry's painted puppets are over the horizon, and Ionesco's automata chorusing "The future is in eggs." Directors, alas, seldom pick up Wilde's hints for a modern style; they tend to keep a uniform tone, ignoring the upsurge of stylisation that makes the characters speak in tune, whistle, chant in chorus until, symmetrical to the last, the pairs are reconciled and fall into each other's arms, exclaiming "Darling!"

Only if this fantastic, balletic/musical effect is achieved (Peter Hall's production went further in this direction than most), can there be the right contrast of tone when Lady Bracknell sweeps in to drag them back to the real world. Despite the fun, that is what is happening when she sets about demolishing one unsuitable engagement and investigating the other with the suspicion induced by the previous day's revelations. "Until yesterday I had` no idea that there were any families or persons whose origin was a Terminus." The wit warms us to her but cannot quite disguise the glacial nature of the snub. The whole tone is harder in this scene, perhaps because she is ruder (she makes Jack "perfectly furious" and "very irritable"); perhaps because repetition slightly reduces the comicality of her routines, making their social unpleasantness more apparent. When she asks "as a matter of form" if Cecily has any fortune and on learning that she has a hundred and thirty thousand pounds in the Funds, finds her "a most attractive young lady," we laugh, of course, but remembering the similar business with Jack, probably feel the edge in the joke more. There is something increasingly alarming as well as droll about her unselfconsciousness: can she really be so unaware or impervious, we wonder, or is she amusing herself with conscious irony when she reflects on Cecily's "really solid qualities" and how they will "last and improve with time," and with supreme effrontery presents herself as the opponent of mercenary marriages:

> Dear child, of course you know that Algernon has nothing but his debts to depend on. But I do not approve of mercenary marriages. When I married Lord Bracknell I had no fortune of any kind. But I never dreamed for a moment of allowing that to stand in my way.

There is no way of penetrating that formidable facade, to find out what goes on behind it (Peter Hall saw the whole action as determined by the will to conceal very strong and real feelings). Wilde planted a time bomb in this character, seemingly set for our time, when there would be a better chance of audiences picking up the serious points the jokes are making—about the "woman question" and marriage. The revelation that Cecily remains a ward till she is thirty-five, for instance, yields much fun, culminating in Lady Bracknell's dry comment that her reluctance to wait till then to be married shows "a somewhat impatient nature." Yet there are sour realities at the back of it, which Wilde does not mean to go unnoticed: we are laughing at (laughing down?) the idea of women being always someone's property, always pawns in the marriage business. Lady Bracknell has made it grotesquely clear that "business" is the word, and she controls society. It is total impasse—the only way out in the other dimension, where Ernest has his equivocal being.

That unpredictable force makes its way back when Canon Chasuble appears, unctuously announcing that he is ready to perform the christenings. It is a wonderful clash of the two worlds. "Algernon, I forbid you to be baptised," booms Lady Bracknell. "Lord Bracknell would be highly displeased if he learned that that was the way in which you wasted your time and money." But the materialist money values, so comically invoked, must give way before the strange inner drive that dictated the christenings; now it brings on Miss Prism, in anxious pursuit of the Canon ("I was told you expected me in the vestry, dear Canon") to be confronted with Lady Bracknell's stony glare and the terrible question: "Prism! Where is that Baby?" The absurd tale of the three-volume novel left in the perambulator and the baby left in the handbag closely parodies attitudes taken in Wilde's other plays. Miss Prism "bows her head in shame," the young men "pretend" to protect the girls from hearing "the details of a terrible public scandal," Jack becomes ever more portentous, requiring Miss Prism to examine *his* handbag carefully to see if it is also hers: "The happiness of more than one

life depends on your answer." The third act was "abominably clever,"
Wilde said. Nothing is cleverer than the way he uses the individualism of
his characters to undermine the old attitudes, overturn them, indeed, by
being irresistibly themselves. Miss Prism cannot keep her head down for
long: one sight of the handbag, and she is away in her own world where
other things, like damage to the lining, are far more important than a sense
of shame:

> Here is the injury it received through the upsetting of a Gower
> Street omnibus in younger and happier days. Here is the stain
> on the lining caused by the explosion of a temperance beverage,
> an incident that occurred at Leamington. . . . The bag is un-
> doubtedly mine. I am delighted to have it so unexpectedly re-
> stored to me. It has been a great inconvenience being without
> it all these years.

No melodrama morality could survive the absurdity of this. Wilde
rolls the whole drama of the "woman with a past," the seduced victim,
the illegitimate child (one critic would include the idea of incest), into the
tiny hilarious episode when Jack tries to embrace Miss Prism, taking her
for his mother. She recoils, exclaiming that she is unmarried, and he makes
his sentimental declaration: "Unmarried! I do not deny that is a serious
blow. But after all, who has the right to cast a stone against one who has
suffered? Cannot repentance wipe out an act of folly? Why should there be
one law for men and another for women? Mother, I forgive you."

Laughing at himself, as well as at the mores of his time, Wilde in this
scene breaks quite free of his century and becomes the "modern" playwright
he wished to be. It is a modern moment for an audience brought up on
Pirandello and Beckett when Jack, turning from one character to another
in search of the truth about himself, is directed by Miss Prism to Lady
Bracknell—"There is the lady who can tell you who you really are"—and
asks her the question that has been causing existential tremors throughout
the play: "Would you kindly inform me who I am?" The answer may be
something we have seen coming but still it causes a shock and it is not
purely comic; it is bound to be a little disturbing to find that his wild and
seemingly casual invention was no more than the truth: he is the brother
of Algernon and his name is Ernest.

The existential hero receives the news "quite calmly"—"I always said
I had a brother! Cecily,—how could you have ever doubted that I had a
brother?"; "I always told you, Gwendolen, my name was Ernest." But it
is surely the calm of one emerging from an experience that has been growing

steadily more manic and disorientating. The crisis of identity is over. Each pair of the quartet fall into each other's arms with the usual symmetry, and Lady Bracknell and Jack share the curtain lines:

> LADY BRACKNELL: My nephew, you seem to be displaying signs of triviality.
>
> JACK: On the contrary, Aunt Augusta, I've now realised for the first time in my life the vital Importance of Being Earnest.

It is the recall to Lady Bracknell's world where "trivial" and "earnest" reverse the values the farce has been asserting. She has won, in a way: the nameless foundling whose very existence was subversive has been assimilated into the Establishment. His father a General, his aunt a Lady: the "decencies of family life" are safe from the revolutionary horrors conjured up by the notion of being "born, or at any rate, bred, in a hand-bag." Yet we cannot be sure. The pun retains its teasing irony to the end. Jack speaks as an actor, looking out to the audience, slyly (never openly) sharing with them the joke closed from Lady Bracknell, that if there is a moral it is only the title for a farce. And the title reminds us that the farce is about being an actor, playing a part, being Ernest by "realising" him, as actors and playwrights realise for their audiences the creations of their fantasy and everybody, in the long run, has to realise his own identity.

Oscar Wilde and the English Epicene

Camille A. Paglia

Oscar Wilde is the premiere documenter of a sexual persona which I call the Androgyne of Manners, embodied in Lord Henry Wotton of *The Picture of Dorian Gray* and in the four young lovers of *The Importance of Being Earnest*. The Androgyne of Manners inhabits the world of the drawing room and creates that world wherever it goes, through manner and mode of speech. The salon is an abstract circle in which male and female, like mathematical ciphers, are equal and interchangeable; personality becomes a sexually undifferentiated formal mask. Rousseau says severely of the eighteenth-century salon, "Every woman at Paris gathers in her apartment a harem of men more womanish than she." The salon is politics by coterie, a city-state or gated forum run on a barter economy of gender exchange.

Elegance, the ruling principle of the salon, dictates that all speech must be wit, in symmetrical pulses of repartee, a malicious stichomythia. Pope's complaint that Lady Mary Wortley Montagu and the epicene Lord Hervey had "too much wit" for him alludes to the icy cruelty of the beau monde, to which moral discourse is alien because it posits the superiority of the inner life to the outer. Sartre says of Genet, "Elegance: the quality of conduct which transforms the greatest quantity of being into appearing." The salon, like the object-realm venerated by the aesthete, is a spectacle of dazzling surfaces—words, faces, and gestures exhibited in a blaze of hard glamour.

Occasionally, Pope was drawn to the idea of spiritual hermaphroditism. But he was deeply hostile to the Androgyne of Manners, whom he

From *Raritan: A Quarterly Review* 4, no. 3 (Winter 1985). © 1985 by *Raritan: A Quarterly Review*.

satirizes as the Amazonian belles and effeminate beaux of *The Rape of the Lock,* because this psychological type is ahistorical in its worship of the ephemeral. The salon is populated by sophisticates of a classical literacy, but its speed of dialogue inhibits deliberation and reflection, recklessly breaking with the past through fashionable irresponsibility. Pope might have said, had the word been available, that the salon was too chic. The Androgyne of Manners—the male feminine in his careless, lounging passivity, the female masculine in her brilliant, aggressive wit—has the profane sleekness of chic.

In the decadent 1890s, before his career abruptly ended in arrest and imprisonment, Wilde was moving towards an Art Nouveau aesthetics. Art Nouveau, then at its height of decorative popularity, is a late phase in the history of style, in many ways analogous to Italian Mannerism. Kenneth Clark says of one of Giambologna's streamlined Mannerist bronzes:

> The goddess of mannerism is the eternal feminine of the fashion plate. A sociologist could no doubt give ready answers why embodiments of elegance should take this somewhat ridiculous shape—feet and hands too fine for honest work, bodies too thin for childbearing, and heads too small to contain a single thought. But elegant proportions may be found in many objects that are exempt from these materialist explanations—in architecture, pottery, or even handwriting. The human body is not the basis of these rhythms but their victim. Where the sense of chic originates, how it is controlled, by what inner pattern we unfailingly recognize it—all these are questions too large and too subtle for a parenthesis. One thing is certain. Chic is not natural. Congreve's Millamant or Baudelaire's dandy warn us how hateful, to serious votaries of chic, is everything that is implied by the word "nature."

Smoothness and elongation, the Mannerist figure is a series of polished ovoids hung on a mannequin's frame. Lord Henry Wotton, with his "long, nervous finger," is an ectomorph, an undulating ribbon of Mannerist Art Nouveau. The ectomorphic line is a suave vertical, repudiating nature by its resistance to gravity, but the Mannerist figure, overcome by worldly fatigue, sinks back toward earth in languorous torsion. The Androgyne of Manners may be seen in complete effete collapse in Henry Lamb's painting of Lytton Strachey turning his back to a window, his long denatured limbs draped over an armchair like wet noodles. Because of its swift verbal genius, however, the Androgyne of Manners is best represented as sleekness and speed. Count Robert de Montesquiou, the decadent model of Huysmans's Des Esseintes and Proust's Charlus, was once described as a "greyhound in evening dress," a phrase we might readily apply to Lord Henry Wotton.

Sleekness in a male is usually a hermaphroditic motive. Cinema, the cardinal medium of modern sexual representation, evokes this theme in its topos of the well-bred English "gentleman," a word of such special connotations that it cannot be perfectly translated into any other language. From the 1930s through the 1950s, movies used actors of this type to illustrate a singular male beauty, witty and polished, uniting sensitivity of response to intense heterosexual glamour: Leslie Howard, Rex Harrison, Cary Grant, David Niven, Michael Wilding, Fred Astaire. The idiomatic representational qualities here are smoothness and elongation, smooth both in manner and appearance, long in ectomorphic height and cranial contour. I think, for instance, of the astounding narrowness of Cary Grant's shiny black evening pumps in *Indiscreet*. The smoothness and elongation of figure are best shown off by a gleaming tuxedo, which signifies a renunciation of masculine hirsutism. The cinematic "gentleman" is always prematurely balding, with swept-back hair at the temples. His receding hairline is sexually expressive, suggesting hermaphroditic gentility, a grace of intellect and emotion. His sleek head is a promise of candor and courtesy, of eroticism without ambivalence or suffering. Smoothness always has an exclusively social meaning: it is nature subdued by the civil made second nature.

In *The Importance of Being Earnest,* the English gentleman, in whom the crudely masculine has been moderated by courtesy, may be seen turning into the Androgyne of Manners, in whom smoothness has become the cold glossiness of a bronze surface, like the "armored look" (*Panzerhaft*) of Bronzino's Mannerist portraits. Meeting and finally mating with their counterparts, the Art Nouveau androgynes of the play speak Wilde's characteristic language, the epicene witticism, analogous to their formal personae in its hardness, smoothness, and elongation. The Wildean epigram, like a Giambologna bronze, is immediately identifiable by a slim spareness, an imperious separateness, and a perverse elegance. Speech in Wilde is made as hard and glittering as possible; it follows the Wildean personality into the visual realm. Normally, it is pictorialism that gives literature a visual character. But there are few metaphors in Wilde and no complex syntactical units. Vocabulary and sentence structure are amazingly simple, arising from the vernacular of the accomplished raconteur. Yet Wilde's bon mots are so condensed that they become *things,* artifacts. Without metaphor, the language leaps into concreteness.

Language in Wilde aspires to an Apollonian hierarchism. His epigrams turn language from the Dionysian Many into the Apollonian One, for as an aphoristic phrase form and conversation stopper, the epigram thwarts real dialogue, cutting itself off from a past and a future in its immediate social context and glorying in its aristocratic solitude. It is the language of the Apollonian lawgiver, arbitrarily assigning form, proportion, and measure. A character in Wilde's *An Ideal Husband* declares, "Women are never disarmed by compliments. Men always are. That is the difference between the sexes." The iron rod of classification is thrust before us—even if it does not fall where expected. In form and in content, the Wildean epigram is a triumph of rhetorical self-containment. No one in English, or probably any other modern language, has produced a series of utterances more mysteriously delimited. The epigram, as practiced in the Renaissance, was a poem of sharply ironic or sententious concluding verses. But the *epigramma* of antiquity was literally an inscription, as on a tombstone. Wilde may therefore be said to have restored the epigram to its original representational character, for his language has a hieroglyphic exactitude and cold rhetorical stoniness, separating itself from its background by the Apollonian incised edge.

In *The Importance of Being Earnest* the courtship of youth and maiden, at the traditional heart of comedy, loses its emotional color in the Wildean transformation of content into form, of soul into surface. Jack Worthing and Algernon Moncrieff, idle gentlemen-about-town, and Gwendolen Fairfax and Cecily Cardew, the well-bred objects of their affections, are all Androgynes of Manners. They have no sex because they have no real sexual feelings. The interactions of the play are governed by the formalities of social life, which emerge with dancelike ritualism. The key phrase of the English fin de siècle was Lionel Johnson's axiom, "Life must be a ritual." In *The Picture of Dorian Gray* Wilde says: "The canons of good society are, or should be, the same as the canons of art. Form is absolutely essential to it. It should have the dignity of a ceremony, as well as its unreality." In *The Importance of Being Earnest* the ceremony of social form is stronger than gender, shaping the personae to its public purpose and turning the internal world into the external.

The play's supreme enforcer of form is Lady Bracknell, who remarks with satisfaction, "We live, I regret to say, in an age of surfaces." In a stage direction to another play, Wilde says of a lord's butler: "The distinction of Phipps is his impassivity. . . . He is a mask with a manner. Of his intellectual or emotional life, history knows nothing. He represents the dominance of form." An optimal performance of *The Importance of Being Earnest* would be a romance of surfaces, male and female alike wearing masks of superb impassivity. The Anthony Asquith film, made in 1952, though it shortens and questionably edits the text, comes close to achieving this. Joan Greenwood's entranced and nearly somnambulistic performance as Gwendolen—slow, stately, and ceremonious—is the brilliant realization of the Wildean aesthetic. But the effort to make Dorothy Tutin's Cecily sympathetic at Gwendolen's expense is sentimentally intrusive, a misreading of the play disordering the symmetry between the two young ladies, twin androgynes who fight each other to a standoff.

Productions of *The Importance of Being Earnest* are often weakened by flights of Forest of Arden lyricism which turn what is sexually ambiguous in Wilde into the conventionally heterosexual. The hieratic purity of the play could best be appreciated if all the women's roles were taken by female impersonators. Language, personality, and behavior should be so hard that the play becomes a spectacle of visionary coldness. The faces should be like glass, without gender or humanity. *The Importance of Being Earnest* takes place in Spenser's Apollonian "world of glas," a realm of glittering, sharp-edged objects. Chapman says of the goddess Ceremony, "all her bodie was / Cleere and transparent as the purest glasse." Gwendolen and Cecily are the goddess Ceremony conversing with herself, her body transparent because she is without an inner life. That Wilde may well have thought of his characters in such terms is suggested in *The Picture of Dorian Gray,* where Lord Henry Wotton longs for "a mask of glass" to shield one from the "sulphurous fumes" of life.

Gwendolen is the first of the women to enact a drama of form. Soliciting Jack to propose to her, she announces in advance that she will accept him but still insists that her bewildered suitor perform the traditional ritual, on his knees. Gwendolen's thoughts never stray from the world of appearances. At the climax of their romantic interlude, she says to Jack, "I hope you will always look at me just like that, especially when there are other people present." This voyeuristic series of observers is a psychosexual topos of decadent late Romanticism, first occurring in 1835 in Gautier's *Mademoiselle de Maupin*. Gwendolen imagines Jack looking at her while she looks at others looking at *them*. As a worshipper of form, Gwendolen craves not emotion but display, the theater of social life.

Gwendolen's self-observing detachment is exhibited by Cecily in precisely the same situation. When Algernon ardently declares his love for her, Cecily replies, "If you will allow me, I will copy your remarks into my diary." Emotion is immediately dispatched into a self-reflexive Mannerist torsion. Going to her writing table, Cecily exhorts her suitor to continue his protestations: "I delight in taking down from dictation." Intimacy is swelled into oratory, and poor Algernon is like Alice grown suddenly too big for the White Rabbit's house. Despite their impending marriage, Cecily declares it quite out of the question for Algernon to see her diary. Nevertheless, it is "meant for publication": "When it appears in volume form I hope you will order a copy." The Sibylline archivist, with professional impartiality, grants no special privileges to her sources of data.

Never for a moment in the play are Gwendolen and Cecily persuasively "female." They are creatures of indeterminate sex who take up the mask of femininity to play a new and provocative role. The dandified Algernon and Jack are simply supporting actors whom the women boldly stage manage. Gwendolen and Cecily are adepts of a dramaturgical alchemy: they are Cerberuses on constant guard to defend the play against encroachment by the internal, which they magically transform into the external. *The Importance of Being Earnest* is one long process of crystallization of the immaterial into the material, of emotion into self-conscious personae. In Shakespeare's volatile Rosalind and Cleopatra, automanipulation of personae arises from a Renaissance abundance of emotion, which flows into a multiplicity of psychodramatic forms. But Wilde's Gwendolen and Cecily inhabit a far more stringently demarcated world, the salon of the Androgyne of Manners, and their personae are radically despiritualized, efflorescences not of psyche but of couture.

Lady Bracknell, too, ruthlessly subordinates persons to form. If Algernon does not come to dinner, "It would put my table completely out," and Lord Bracknell will be exiled upstairs. In one of Wilde's most wonderful lines, Lady Bracknell rebukes Jack for being an orphan: "To lose one parent, Mr. Worthing, may be regarded as a misfortune; to lose both looks like carelessness." Matters of form are uppermost, in death as in life. The emotional intensities of Victorian bereavement are cancelled. Nothing is of interest but the public impression. Once again there is the late Romantic stress upon visual cognition: "may be *regarded* as a misfortune;" "*looks* like carelessness." Every event occurs with naked visibility on a vast, flat expanse; life is a play scrutinized by a ring of appraising eyes. This illustrates one of Wilde's central principles, as cited by Dorian Gray: "To become the spectator of one's own life is to escape the suffering of life." Late Romantic spectatorship is an escape from suffering because all affect is transferred from the emotional and tangible into the visual: no wounds can pierce the glassy body of the Wildean androgyne. The self is without a biological or historical identity. Self-originating, it has no filial indebtedness. A parent is merely a detail of social heraldry. To lose both parents, therefore, is not tragedy but negligence, like tipping the tea service into the trashbin.

The liturgy of the religion of form of which Lady Bracknell is a communicant, and in which she has instructed her daughter Gwendolen, is determined by fashion, whose bible is any one of "the more expensive monthly magazines." Lady Bracknell declares, "Style largely depends on the way the chin is worn. They are worn very high, just at present." The chin is imperiously "worn" like an article of clothing because the human figure is merely decorative, like the mummy's foot which serves as a paperweight in a Gautier tale. There is a latent surrealism here, for once the chin, like the eyebrow of Gautier's hieratic Cleopatra, has been detached from the body by decadent partition, there is no reason why it cannot be worn elsewhere—on the shoulder, perhaps, or hip. Gwendolen, requesting Cecily's permission to examine her through a lorgnette (Cecily graciously makes the expected late romantic reply, "I am very fond of being looked at"), boasts that her mother "has brought me up to be extremely short-sighted." The body is sculpted at the whim of fashion, responding to its commands with plastic ductility.

At the tea table, Gwendolen declines Cecily's offer of sugar: "No thank you. Sugar is not fashionable any more." To the choice of cake or bread and butter, she replies ("in a bored manner"), "Bread and butter, please. Cake is rarely seen at the best houses nowadays." For Gwendolen, tastiness is irrelevant, since the body has no needs in the world of form. Sugar and cake are items of decor, marks of caste by which one group separates itself from a lower group. Personal preference is renounced for hierarchical conformity. And note that cake is "rarely *seen,*" not eaten—its status is visual and not gustatory. Gwendolen is an Androgyne of Manners rapidly approaching the android. She is so completely the product of fashion that she is a machine, seeking myopically by maternal edict, eating, drinking, hearing, thinking, and speaking by preprogrammed desire. Mallarmé says, "Fashion is the goddess of appearances." Fashion is the divinity of this world of form, which Lady Bracknell and Gwendolen uphold with apostolic fervor.

The literary term "high comedy" is often rather loosely applied to any comedy of manners that does not descend to broad verbal or physical humor. I would argue that the most advanced high comedy is a ceremoniously mannered "presentation of self," the style of *The Importance of Being Earnest,* as most splendidly exemplified by Gwendolen. Indeed, in Gwendolen Fairfax, Wilde has reached the generic limit of high comedy. Gwendolen's self-hierarchization is so extreme that other characters are virtually dispensable, for they impinge on her only feebly and peripherally. But without at least two characters, drama as a genre cannot exist. When Gwendolen speaks it is not to others as much as to herself or to some abstract choir of celestial observers. Like the picture of Dorian Gray, which is not content to remain in its assigned place and rejects its entelechy, she seems ready to abandon drama for some extrageneric destination. Here is Wilde's greatest departure from the Restoration dramatists, for he detaches the witticism from repartee, that is, from social relationship. The Wildean witticism is a Romantic phenomenon in its proud isolationism. In this mode of high comedy there is an elaborately formal or ritualistic display of the persona, indeed a brandishing of it, like an aegis. The practitioner is in a double relation to the self, acting and also observing. But more importantly, there is a distinct trace of late Romantic "connoisseurship": the self is the subject of decadent studiousness and scholarship.

Let us examine several of Gwendolen's incomparable utterances, with their unyielding uniformity of tone. Late in the play she says, "I never change, except in my affections." This could serve as a darkly ironic caption to Walter Pater's decadent "Mona Lisa." But what Gwendolen means is that, just as once might expect, she is rigidly punctilious in formal and external matters, while emotional events are beneath notice, flotsam and jetsam aimlessly adrift. Observe how she "brandishes" her personality, flaunting her faults with triumphant self-love. Her speech always has a hard, even, relentless, and yet rhetorically circumscribed character, as in her first words in the play:

> ALGERNON: Dear me, you are smart!
> GWENDOLEN: I am always smart! Am I not, Mr. Worthing?
> JACK: You're quite perfect, Miss Fairfax.
> GWENDOLEN: Oh! I hope I am not that. It would leave no
>   room for developments, and I intend to develop in many
>   directions.

If we were to speak of a psychodramatic "music," then in this last clause we are hearing the monody of a Gautierian contralto, the husky self-plea-suring of hermaphrodite autonomy. Identical intonations are present in two other of Gwendolen's remarks. At one point she gratuitously informs her suitor, "in fact, I am never wrong." And in the last act, as Jack struggles to regain her alienated affections, she says to him, "I have the gravest doubts upon the subject. But I intend to crush them." Such lines must be properly read—with slow, resonant measure—in order to appreciate their intractable severity. "I intend to develop in many directions": there is an extraordinarily distinctive sound to this in British diction, flat, formal, and sonorous, forbidding with self-command. Note the way personality is *distributed* throughout the sentence, filling the narrow channel of its syntax with a dense silvery fluid, acrid and opaque. Gwendolen's willful, elegantly linear sentences fit her like a glove. Smooth with Mannerist spareness, they carry not an extra ounce of rhetorical avoirdupois. There is no Paterian mistiness in Gwendolen. She overtly relishes her personality, caressing its hard edges, which are echoed in the brazen contours of her sentences. In this doyenne of Art Nouveau worldliness, Wilde has created a definitively modern self-hood, exposed, limited, and unsentimental, cold as urban geometry.

Above all his characters, it is Gwendolen whom Wilde has charged with creating an Apollonian dramatic language. Her speech, like Wilde's epicene witticisms, has a metallic self-enclosed terseness. She spends her words with haughty frugality for the same reason that Spenser's Belphoebe dashes off in the middle of sentences: the Apollonian is a mode of self-sequestration. The bon mot in general is jealous of its means, prizing brevity above all. It is a kind of sacramental display, permitting the self to be seen only in epiphanic flashes, like the winking of a camera shutter. These spasms of delimitation are attempts to defy the temporal character of speech or narrative, turning sequences of words into discrete *objets*. Ideas are never developed in the Apollonian style because of its antipathy to internality. Instead, as we find in Gwendolen and in the classic maliciously witty Androgyne of Manners of the salon, language is used confrontationally, as a distancing weapon, like a flaming sword. Gwendolen's self-exhibiting utterances follow the principle of *frontality* in painting and sculpture, which, as Arnold Hauser observes, is intrinsic to "all courtly and courteous art." Abjuring the modesty of the unmarried maiden, the potent Gwendolen turns herself full-face to her suitor, bathing him with a rain of hierarchical emissions.

Admiration of *The Importance of Being Earnest* is widespread, but discussion of the play is scarce and slight. Critics seem to have accepted Wilde's own description of it—"exquisitely trivial, a delicate bubble of fancy." Scholarship has never distinguished itself in studying this kind of high comedy, with its elusive "sophistication." Frye-style myth criticism, for example, can do little with *The Importance of Being Earnest*. From the point of view of decadent late Romanticism, however, there is scarcely a line in the play which fails to yield rich implications.

Here are two examples. In the midst of her dispute with Cecily, Gwendolen declares, "I never travel without my diary. One should always have something sensational to read in the train." The latter sentence comes as a surprise, for ordinarily one travels with a diary not to read but to write in it. Gwendolen, however, as an Apollonian androgyne, does not keep a journal for self-examination—inwardness always being distasteful—but for self-display. To read one's diary as if it were a novel is to regard one's life as spectacle, which Wilde of course advocates. Gwendolen contemplates her life with appreciative detachment, acting both as objet d'art and late Romantic connoisseur. Reading is normally a medium of expansion of personal experience; one reads to learn what one does not know. Here, however, reading is an act of Romantic solipsism: Gwendolen reads not to enlarge but to condense herself. Far from Emily Dickinson's mobile frigate, a book has become a mirror in which one sees only one's own face. The diary is a self-portrait. Hence Gwendolen reading her diary in a train compartment is exactly like Dorian Gray standing before his picture in the locked room. Both are performing their devotions to the hierarchized self.

The life which this diary records is, according to Gwendolen, "sensational," a source of public scandal and eroticized fascination. But to find one's own life sensational is to be aroused by oneself. The eyes, as always in late Romanticism, are sexual agents: Gwendolen reading her diary is lost in autoerotic skeptophilia, a titillation of the eye. If books can corrupt, and we know from *The Picture of Dorian Gray* that they can, then it is possible to be corrupted by one's own diary. To be corrupted by oneself is a perfect pattern of sexual solipsism, like Goethe's twisting Venetian acrobat Bettina, self-delectating and self-devirginizing. Gwendolen is an uroboros of amorous self-study, an Art Nouveau serpent devouring herself. Train reading is casual reading, a way to pass time with minimal effort. The life recorded and contemplated in the diary is therefore reduced in significance, trivialized: it is simply a series of sensational incidents without moral meaning.

Reading one's diary like a novel implies that one has forgotten what is in it. It demonstrates a lack of moral memory characteristic of the Decadent in general. In Wilde's *A Woman of No Importance,* Lord Illingworth declares, "No woman should have a memory. Memory in a woman is the beginning of dowdiness." The internal erodes the perfection of surfaces. In *An Ideal Husband,* Sir Robert Chiltern says of an antagonist, "She looks like a woman with a past," to which Lord Goring replies, "Most pretty women do." But as we see from Gwendolen's relations with her diary, the person with a past has no past. The self is a tabula rasa open only to sensationalized Paterian "impressions." There is no moral incrementation; experience corrupts, but it does not instruct. In *The Picture of Dorian Gray* Lord Henry Wotton reflects, "Experience was of no ethical value. It was merely the name men gave to their mistakes." Reading one's diary is a diversion of the "late" phase of culture. Memory is inhibited precisely because one has done *too much,* like Pater's "Mona Lisa," fatigued by history.

Her information retrieval system blocked by sensory overload, the robotlike Gwendolen is a stranger to herself, a stranger-lover.

Gwendolen never travels without her diary because it is her familiar, the inseparable escort which enables her to keep herself in a state of externalization. This is one of many traits she shares with Cecily, who uses her diary to similar effect, as we saw in the proposal scene, where Cecily instantly petrifies Algernon's sentiments midair, as if engraving them upon stone tablets. Gwendolen's diary, again like the picture of Dorian Gray, is a repository of the soul which she is able to carry about with her like a hatbox, preserving her soulless Apollonian purity. The diary is also a chronicle, the testament of her cult of the self. For both the high and late Romantic, a diary is a personal cosmogony, a book of first and last things.

Hence it can be seen that Wilde's witticisms contain a wealth of unsuspected meaning. Even his most apparently nonsensical *boutades* are late Romantic gestures. For example, Lady Bracknell attempts to terminate the stormy scene at the Manor House by declaring to Gwendolen, "Come, dear, we have already missed five, if not six, trains. To miss any more might expose us to comment on the platform." These bizarre lines have that air of skewed lunatic certainty we know from Lewis Carroll, who I believe strongly influenced Wilde. What is Lady Bracknell saying? Missing a train, even "five, if not six" (a studied Decadent enumeration) normally has only private and not public consequences. In the looking-glass world of form, however, failure to adhere to plan is an affront to natural law, bringing murmurs of complaint from passersby. But how do others learn of one's deviation from a train schedule? Since everything is visible in this landscape of externals, and since the mental life of these androgynes, like their bodies, has a glassy transparency, their intention may be said to precede them, like a town crier, alerting the populace to their tardiness. In its visionary materialism, *The Importance of Being Earnest* reverts to the Homeric world of allegorized psychic phenomena, in which the enraged Achilles feels Athena tugging at his hair. If we characterized Lady Bracknell's remark in naturalistic terms, we would have to speak of a megalomaniacal paranoia: she imagines a general consciousness of their every move; everyone knows what they are doing and thinking. But this is a development of aristocratic worldliness. Fashionable life, as Proust attests, does indeed take place before the unblinking eyes of *le tout Paris*.

"To miss any more might expose us to comment on the platform": Lady Bracknell exists in a force field of visual sightlines. Like Gautier's chaste Queen Nyssia, tainted by the gaze of another, Lady Bracknell fears being "exposed" to infection, in this case an infection of words. Barthes says of the sadomasochistic relations in Sade's novels, "The master is he who speaks . . . ; the object is he who is silent." Lady Bracknell will lose caste if she is subject to public "comment." Her hierarchical dominance will drain from her, like divine ichor. The scene of shame which she envisions on the railway platform is one of ritual exposure, like Hawthorne's Hester Prynne braving public scorn on the town scaffold. In Wilde's world, of course, crime is not sin but bad form.

The Importance of Being Earnest was the last thing Wilde wrote before his fall. Its opening night coincided with the initiation of the Marquess of Queensberry's most virulent campaign against him, and the play continued to be performed, to great acclaim, during his two trials. Now it is a strange fact that Wilde's passage to prison was a terrible fulfillment of this remark by Lady Bracknell. In De Profundis, written in Reading Gaol, Wilde recalls:

> On November 13th, 1895, I was brought down here from London. From two o'clock till half-past two on that day I had to stand on the centre platform of Clapham Junction in convict dress, and handcuffed, for the world to look at. . . . When people saw me they laughed. Each train as it came up swelled the audience. Nothing could exceed their amusement. That was, of course, before they knew who I was. As soon as they had been informed they laughed still more. For half an hour I stood there in the grey November rain surrounded by a jeering mob.
>
> For a year after that was done to me I wept every day at the same hour and for the same space of time.

Lady Bracknell's railway platform was to be the site of Wilde's greatest humiliation. Who can doubt that the imagination can shape reality to its will? So close are these two scenes of ritual exposure that one wonders whether Wilde's memory of Clapham Junction was not a hallucination, a variation on a fictive theme in the solitude and squalor of prison. But granting its truth, it is another example of Wilde's shamanistic power to bring his own imaginative projections into being. Publication of The Picture of Dorian Gray produced Lord Alfred Douglas, the beautiful boy as destroyer, who brought Wilde to his ruin. Clapham Junction came as the agonizing materialization of Wilde's principle of life as "spectacle." The entire late Romantic tradition of concentrated visual experience reaches a disastrous climax on that railway platform, and it ends there, with Wilde the dizzy center of the visible world, like the Ancient Mariner the focus of cosmic wrath, here taking the unbearable form of laughter. The comedian, losing control of his genre, is devoured by the audience.

The epicene witticism has received little attention partly because it is sexually heterodox and partly because it does not fit into received critical categories. Thus Wilde's plays are suitable for explication while his conversation is not. But the Androgyne of Manners, of which Wilde was his own best example, makes an art of the spoken word. With his radical formalism, Wilde created an original language which I will call the *monologue extérieur*.

The salon dialogue of the Androgyne of Manners is a duel of "cutting" remarks. Language is used aggressively as an instrument of masculine warfare designed to slash, stab, pierce, and penetrate. Dorian Gray says to Lord Henry Wotton, "You cut life to pieces with your epigrams." It is no coincidence that terms describing a witty exchange—thrust, parry, riposte, repartee—are drawn from swordplay. The close interrelations of language and martial contention in Western culture are demonstrated by fencing parlance which speaks of a "conversation" or "phrase" of action. In other words, a fencing match is imagined as a sequence of competitive speech. It is plain how a woman of the salon who commands this sharp, challenging rhetoric is masculinized into an Androgyne of Manners. The male Androgyne of Manners achieves his hermaphroditism by combining aggressive language with a feminine manner, graceful and languid, archly flirtatious and provocative. The persona which Wilde projects in his epicene witticisms is a conflation of masculine intimidation and attack with feminine seduction and allure.

To "cut" someone is to wound him, but it is also to sever social connections with him. This duality is the subject of a pun by Lewis Carroll, when Alice is introduced to the leg of mutton:

> "May I give you a slice?" she said, taking up the knife and fork, and looking from one Queen to the other.
> "Certainly not," the Red Queen said, very decidedly: "It isn't etiquette to cut any one you've been introduced to. Remove the joint!"

Wilde's witticisms operate by a systematic "cutting," separating the self from communality and withdrawing it into an aristocratic sequestration. In *The Importance of Being Earnest* Wilde makes language into a mode of hierarchical placement. It is a series of psychodramatic gestures, each remark asserting a caste location with regard to some other person or class of person. The speakers are constantly positioning themselves at fixed distances from others. This even occurs, as we have seen, in the marriage proposals, where the heroines of the play befuddle the heroes by ceremonial demarcations, exclamatory bulletins of incipient intimacy, which they narrate like play-by-play sportscasters. To paraphrase: "We will shortly be intimate"; "We are now being intimate"; "Pray continue to be intimate." The Wildean heroine is a hierarchical commentator, plotting the relations of personae upon a mental map.

The use of language as signs of placement is often overt, as in the tea table dispute between the young ladies.

> CECILY: When I see a spade I call it a spade.
> GWENDOLEN (satirically): I am glad to say that I have never
> seen a spade. It is obvious that our social spheres have
> been widely different.

In this literalization of metaphor, a characteristic Wildean materialization, a spade becomes, like sugar or cake, a calibrator of caste. Gwendolen glories in her self-expanded hierarchical distance from Cecily. Such language appears everywhere in *The Importance of Being Earnest*. For example, the play opens with Algernon playing the piano: "I don't play accurately—anyone can play accurately—but I play with wonderful expression." "Anyone can play accurately": this self-absolving and demonstrably untrue premise, like a ladder leaned against a wall, stretches a great chain of being before our eyes, with Algernon exulting over the mass of the many from a topmost rung of aesthetical "sensibility." The technique is used throughout Wilde. His polemical spokesman in "The Critic as Artist" says, "When people agree with me I always feel that I must be wrong." And a character in *An Ideal Husband* says, "Only dull people are brilliant at breakfast." Rhetorical energy is entirely directed toward social differentiation and segregation. Wilde was committed to an Apollonian enterprise—to create hierarchy through wit, ennobling himself, like the self-naming Balzac, through a magisterial persona construction.

Hence the epicene witticism is a language of hierarchical command in sexually aberrant or rather sexually denatured form. Wilde's "pointed" hierarchical style ultimately descends from the eighteenth century and in particular from Pope, whose poetry Wilde vociferously disliked. Brigid Brophy asserts: "Wilde's vehicle, the epigram, is in fact an adaptation of the logical axiom and the scientific definition. The Irish—perhaps originally theological—habit of paradox . . . is (like the paradoxical mysteries of Christian theology itself) nothing else than an exposure of the ambivalence concealed in our morality." But more precisely, Wilde's epigrams, which so impede the quickness of Restoration repartee, have acquired their substantiveness from eighteenth-century generalization. It is his power of generalization which gives Wilde's writing its permanent distinction. A modern play in the Wildean manner, Noel Coward's *Private Lives,* has only one truly Wildean line: "Certain women should be struck regularly, like gongs." And even this generalizing axiom is a vulgarization of Wilde, in whom contemplativeness is never distorted by action.

It was Pope who first made poetic beauty out of philosophy, devising a discursive style of elegant containment and high finish. Pope's rhetorical and social assumptions were transmitted to Wilde, apparently against his will, by the conservative Jane Austen, in whom we first detect Wilde's distinctive voice, tart, bantering, and lucid. Consider, for example, the great opening sentence of *Emma*:

> Emma Woodhouse, handsome, clever, and rich, with a comfortable home and happy disposition, seemed to unite some of the best blessings of existence; and had lived nearly twenty-one years in the world with very little to distress or vex her.

There is a delicate play of modern irony around the psychological edges of this sentence which is almost impossible to arrest and define. It is a meteorological disturbance or atmospheric rippling, an undulating vocal convection. Philosophically, Jane Austen's novels, although contemporaneous with high Romanticism, affirm the eighteenth-century world view, with its neoclassic endorsement of the sexually normative. Only in *Emma* can we find anything sexually ambivalent—in Emma's infatuation with Harriet—and even there it is slight and discreet.

Wilde diverts Jane Austen's comedy into the epicene first through his own character as a decadent late Romantic. Eighteenth-century wit is aligned with nature, from which Wilde makes a late Romantic swerve. But this antinaturism enables Wilde to eliminate the sexual specificities of Restoration comedy. Human lusts no longer exist in *The Importance of Being Earnest*. Even Algernon's perpetual hunger is an angelic appetite, for the characters of the play feed on things insubstantial as manna: bread and butter, cucumber sandwiches, muffins, crumpets, and tea cake. They are like the Bread-and-butter-fly of *Through the Looking-Glass*, whose head is a lump of sugar and who lives on weak tea with cream. Wilde uses Jane Austen to *clarify* high comedy, stripping away the broad and farcical elements which had been present in it since Shakespeare. There are no longer any low-comic or crudely dialectal interludes. Even the secondary characters of *The Importance of Being Earnest* are erudite verbalists. (MISS PRISM: "I spoke horticulturally. My metaphor was drawn from fruits.") Wilde has pruned and simplified high comedy by eighteenth-century standards of taste, decorum, and correctness.

But there is a second influence in Wilde's epicene transformation of

Jane Austen. He is aided in this project by the one wit who stands between himself and her—Lewis Carroll. It is Carroll who detaches English comedy from the ethical (which it displays even in the bawdy Restoration plays, with their virtuous finales) and prepares it for its definitive amoralization at the hands of Wilde. After Wilde, this genre of glittering high comedy is confined to the epicene and can be practiced only by sex-crossing imaginations—Ronald Firbank, Noel Coward, Cole Porter. The sexual ambiguity in Lewis Carroll is not textually overt; that development was to be implemented by Wilde. But it is perfectly evident in his life. His friends and biographers speak of his long hair and "curiously womanish face," his fascination with little girls, his detestation of boys, which was "an aversion, almost amounting to terror." Carroll's self-identification was thoroughly feminine.

The dramatic force of the *Alice* books rests upon the stability of the Victorian social structure which invisibly supports them. Alice is an imperialist of custom. Thrust into an irrational dreamworld, she remains serene and self-assured, a model of well-bred composure. In her firm sense of the limits of appropriate behavior, she is twin to that menagerie of potentates, human and animal, who chide her for transgressions of mysterious local codes of conduct. There is even a surprising cultural kinship between Alice and her chief critic, the fierce Red Queen, whom Carroll elsewhere describes as "formal and strict, . . . the concentrated essence of all governesses." But the Red Queen is a governess only insofar as the governess is the first and most immediate representative of the hierarchical in the lives of English children, ruling as a regent in the name of society.

Carroll did not, I contend, hold the Romantic or modern view that social laws are artificial and false. On the contrary, he took an Apollonian pleasure in them, admiring and cherishing them as he did the equations and theorems he manipulated as an academic mathematician. One of the first pieces Carroll published as a young man at Oxford was a list of nonsensical principles, "Hints for Etiquette; or, Dining Out Made Easy."

I

In proceeding to the dining-room, the gentleman gives one arm to the lady he escorts—it is unusual to offer both.

III

To use a fork with your soup, intimating at the same time to your hostess that you are reserving the spoon for the beefsteaks, is a practice wholly exploded.

VI

The method of helping roast turkey with two carving-forks is practicable, but deficient in grace.

VII

We do not recommend the practice of eating cheese with a knife and fork in one hand, and a spoon and wine-glass in the other; there is a kind of awkwardness in the action which no amount of practice can entirely dispel.

VIII

As a general rule, do not kick the shins of the opposite gentleman under the table, if personally unacquainted with him; your pleasantry is liable to be misunderstood—a circumstance at all times unpleasant.

It would be a typically modern error to assume that this is an essay in "debunking," that Carroll is reducing manners to the absurd in order to demonstrate the fictiveness of social custom. But everything we know about Carroll's private and public deportment shows him to be an inflexible advocate of order. A contemporary speaks of the "rigid rule of his own life," his fixed daily routine. Another says that he was "austere, shy, precise, . . . watchfully tenacious of his dignity, stiffly conservative in political, theological, social theory, his life mapped out in squares like Alice's landscape."

The evidence suggests that the rules and manners of "Hints for Etiquette" and the *Alice* books draw much of their force from Carroll's belief in their tradition-consecrated and even a priori character. Nearly all the comedy of Carroll's work arises from a natively English love of formality and ceremony. There is a tonality of wit in Carroll which has no parallel in premodern literature but which appears throughout Virginia Woolf, particularly in her masterpiece, *To the Lighthouse*. Note the similarities of voice, for example, between Carroll's "Hints for Etiquette" and this passage from a letter to Victoria Sackville-West in which Woolf reviews the comments roused by her newly bobbed hair:

1. Virginia is completely spoilt by her shingle.
2. Virginia is completely made by her shingle.
3. Virginia's shingle is quite unnoticeable.

These are the three schools of thought on this important subject. I have bought a coil of hair, which I attach by a hook. It falls into the soup, and is fished out on a fork.

This sophisticated comic style, with its subtlety of ironic inflection, seems to be produced in England by some unexplored interaction between language and persona.

The deep structure of such passages is as follows. An excessive or unforeseen event occurs within the strict confines of convention. The dining table is the favored locus of display, as the arena of daily domestic ritual. However, the incident elicits no reaction, or only a muted one. All personae remain in a state of dignified flat affect, restoring and preserving the rule of normality. The highest English comedy is predicated on a Wildean impassivity of countenance. One can see in the Woolf letter, in fact, how three diverse reactions are allowed to cancel each other out, cleverly effecting a return to stasis. The energy deflected from reaction flows into the social structure of the occasion, which is felt with architectural solidity, vibrating with public power.

Lewis Carroll covertly introduced an epicene element into English humor which, consolidated by Wilde, has continued in force to the present. It took immediate cultural root because of certain abiding features of upper-class English personality, foremost of which is the hermaphroditic type of the "gentleman," upon which I have already remarked. English society has also been noted for a toleration of eccentricity, a proliferation of sadomasochistic erotica, and a high incidence of male homosexuality stimulated by the monasticism of public-school and university life.

Lewis Carroll, in his two strange and inexhaustible books, synthesized several of the most potent elements in English high culture: wit, hierarchy, and spiritual hermaphroditism. After Carroll, English comedy, in literature and in educated dialogue, often tends towards the absurd and incongruous, in which there is always a shadow of the epicene. What Carroll did was first to invent a nonchthonian animism, giving Romantic nature a social voice. The *Alice* books are a din of creatures, speaking as uncompromising social hierarchs. There is no "tenderness" in Carroll's characters, save in the bumbling and ineffectual, like the feeble White Knight. All are sharp, forceful personalities, nodes of aggressive selfhood. The *Alice* books, like *The Importance of Being Earnest,* are glutted with rules of behavior, which pop up at the most improbable moments. Formality is the preeminent principle in Carroll, governing not only the narrative design (a pack of cards structures the first book and a chessboard the second), but also the psychodramatic style of the characters, a punctilious ritualism not unlike Carroll's own. The Red Queen's draconian championship of manners is merely the most blatant of the ritual formulas of Carroll's animistic world, and manners are the language of the hierarchical. Veblen remarks: "Manners

. . . are symbolical and conventionalised survivals representing former acts
of dominance or of personal service or of personal contact. In large part
they are an expression of status,—a symbolic pantomime of mastery on the
one hand and of subservience on the other."

It is the ancient history of manners as articulations of power which
energizes the climactic confrontation between Gwendolen and Cecily, the
center not only of *The Importance of Being Earnest* but probably of Wilde's
entire oeuvre. In a tableau of brilliant formal beauty, a tea table is made
the scene of a ferocious wargame, with manners the medium of ritual
advance and retreat. Gwendolen and Cecily manipulate their personae with
chill virtuosity. Nowhere else in the play is it more evident that the gender
of the Androgyne of Manners is purely artificial, that "femininity" in the
salon is simply a principle of decorum shared equally by male and female.
The escalating emotion of the conversation between Gwendolen and Cecily
is entirely absorbed by the ceremonial framework and by the formality of
their social masks.

> CECILY (*rather shy and confidingly*): Dearest Gwendolen, there is
> no reason why I should make a secret of it to you. Our
> little county newspaper is sure to chronicle the fact next
> week. Mr. Ernest Worthing and I are engaged to be
> married.
>
> GWENDOLEN (*quite politely, rising*): My darling Cecily, I think
> there must be some slight error. Mr. Ernest Worthing is
> engaged to me. The announcement will appear in the
> *Morning Post* on Saturday at the latest.
>
> CECILY (*very politely, rising*): I am afraid you must be under
> some misconception. Ernest proposed to me exactly ten
> minutes ago. (*Shows diary.*)
>
> GWENDOLEN (*examines diary through her lorgnette carefully*): It is
> very curious, for he asked me to be his wife yesterday
> afternoon at 5:30. If you would care to verify the
> incident, pray do so. (*Produces diary of her own.*)

Each gesture, each rhetorical movement is answered by a symmetrical
countermovement of balletic grandeur. Language becomes increasingly
elaborate, in baroque convolutions of ironic restraint: "It would distress
me more than I can tell you, dear Gwendolen, if it caused you any mental
or physical anguish, but I feel bound to point out that since Ernest proposed
to you he clearly has changed his mind." There is no hysteria, or even
excitement. The immovable wills of the two young women press so fiercely

against the social limits of the moment that the hierarchical structure of manners leaps into visibility, another of Wilde's characteristic materializations. Stylization and ritualism approach the Oriental. The scene is a Japanese tea ceremony in which gracious self-removal has yielded to barely concealed Achillean strife.

It was Lewis Carroll who made this greatest of Wildean episodes possible. In Carroll, manners and social laws are disconnected from humane or "civilizing" values. They have a mathematical beauty but no moral meaning: they are absurd. But this absurdity is predicated not on some democratic notion of their relativism but on their arbitrary, divine incomprehensibility. In the *Alice* books, manners are meaningless, but they still retain their hierarchical force; they are Veblen's "pantomime" of mastery and subservience. Wilde, influenced by Carroll, appropriates his view of the mechanisms of social power and sets it into a much larger system of aristocratic presuppositions derived partly from his self-identification as a Baudelairean late Romantic (always reactionary and antiliberal) and partly from his reading of English drama, in which aristocracy is one of the leading moral "ideas."

In the century of the middle class, Wilde reaffirms aristocratic *virtù*, fabricating it out of its accumulated meanings in English literature. *The Importance of Being Earnest* is a reactionary political poem which takes aristocratic style as the supreme embodiment of life as art. Through its masquelike use of manners as social spectacle, the play seeks out the crystallized idea or Platonic form of aristocracy, which resides in rank, in the ascending gradations of the great chain of being. Wilde's bon mots bring an Apollonian world into being: language and ceremony unite to take the hierarchical to its farthest dazzling point, until it appears as form without content, like the icy latticework of a snowflake. Thus it is that the characters of *The Importance of Being Earnest,* and especially the women, have abnormal attitudes, reactions, and customs and embark upon sequences of apparently irrational thought, for they are a strange hierarchical race, the *aristoi.*

Wilde's play is inspired by the glamour of aristocracy alone, divorced from social function. In this it is quite unlike Augustan literature, which celebrates Queen Anne for her wisdom and stability of rule. In Wilde no collective benefits flow from throne or court, where the upper class is preoccupied with fashionable diversions. No contemporary regime is eulogized, no past one nostalgically commemorated. Indeed, social order has no legal, economic, or military aspects whatever; it is entirely divorced from practical reality. Class structure in Wilde exists as *art,* as pure form. This markedly contrasts with Ulysses' sermon on "degree" in Shakespeare's

Troilus and Cressida: in *The Importance of Being Earnest* order is admired not because it is right or just but because it is beautiful. In fact, order here makes no intellectual sense at all; in Carrollian terms, it is absurd. Hence it is an error, and a common one, to say that Wilde is "satirizing" Lady Bracknell, making her ridiculous in her haughty presumptions. Lady Bracknell is beautiful *because* she is absurd. Aristocracy in *The Importance of Being Earnest* satisfies aesthetic and not moral demands. The world of the play is *kosmios,* well-ordered and comely. And that it is ruled by the chic makes perfect sense when one realizes that the etymological descent of this word resembles that of *cosmetic* from *cosmos,* for the French *chic* is apparently a version of the German *schick,* meaning taste, elegance, and order.

Outside his art, Wilde found himself in the same quandary as Coleridge and Swinburne, anxiously attempting apologia and moral revision of their daemonic poems. Thus Wilde declares in "The Soul of Man under Socialism": "All authority is quite degrading. It degrades those who exercise it, and it degrades those over whom it is exercised." Wilde was torn between his instinctive hierarchism as an Apollonian idealist and the liberalism to which he was impelled by the miseries of being homosexual in a Christian society. This led him into glaring self-contradictions, as in the testimony at his two trials.

The Wildean epicene unites the great English dramatic theme of aristocracy with late Romantic aestheticism and decadence. The first step in this process is Wilde's severance of the hierarchical social values of the eighteenth century and Jane Austen from the ideal of commonweal. The second step is his sexual volatilization of English wit. The bantering rhetoric of the celibate Jane Austen and Lewis Carroll becomes epicene in Wilde because of his sexual experience, with its shift into decadence. Works of epicene wit are typically dominated by image—a tyranny of the visual— and by scandal and gossip. There is little scandal or gossip in Lewis Carroll because the *Alice* books have no sexual "free energy": Carroll is an annalist of aggression but not of eroticism. In Wilde, however, gossip is a primary force, intensifying the aura of glamour by which prestige is measured in the salon. The erotic excitation of scandal and gossip produces the volatility of Wildean wit, aiding its transformation into the epicene. Words cast off their moral meanings and escape into the sexually transcendental, leaving only vapor trails of flirtation and frivolity.

Wilde and the Evasion of Principle

Joseph Loewenstein

> *Charming, quite charming. And, do you know, from time to time it reminded me of a play I once wrote called* The Importance of Being Earnest.
>
> Oscar Wilde, to the actor-manager George Alexander, after the first performance of *The Importance of Being Earnest*

There is more than a little risk in this enterprise. Though Wilde was himself a famous, if not to say notorious, critic, he was also unkind enough to remark on the inevitable folly of public pronouncement. "How appalling," he writes, "is that ignorance which is the inevitable result of imparting opinions." I will not be the first critic to go on about *The Importance of Being Earnest,* while appearing steadily to descend the evolutionary chain in the course of doing so. The first person to feel this way was William Archer—one of the few drama critics whom Wilde seems to have respected. Then Archer reviewed the play, he too began from the vantage of self-pity: "What can a poor critic do with a play which raises no principle, whether of art of morals . . . and is nothing but an absolutely wilful expression of an irrepressibly witty personality?" Shaw had taken just such a tack in a review of Wilde's previous play, a review written for the *Saturday Review* a few weeks before *Earnest* opened, in which he observed that Wilde had the peculiar "property of making his critics dull."

Whether or not one sympathizes with my predicament or with Shaw's, one should, I think, sympathize with Archer's. He was the champion of *serious* Victorian drama, which meant, for him, being a champion of Ibsen's plays and of those early plays by Shaw which *looked* like Ibsen's plays only

From *The South Atlantic Quarterly* 84, no. 4 (Autumn 1985). © 1985 by Duke University Press.

without the snow. He liked Wilde's plays, though; he couldn't help liking them—this is no doubt why Wilde liked his reviews—but his own principles kept him from knowing what to say about them.

The temptation not to say anything about such a play as *Earnest* is strong; and the temptation not to say anything *serious* about such a play is exceptionally strong. Yet one resists the temptation on Wilde's own orders, for oddly enough his own lectures, plays, novels, and conversation are full of insistences that criticism shares the mission of art, that art must be critical and criticism creative. I could sum up what my own thinly creative contribution will be here, but that would be inartistic. Even to hint darkly that I think the play to have been very aptly named or to reveal that this essay ought properly be entitled "Wilde as Moralist" is to give too much of the game away. Wilde once wrote that the primary function of criticism was "to deepen a book's mystery." Mystery is more difficult to generate than many readers think, but in his own critical writing Wilde overcomes this particular difficulty by avoiding straightforward pronouncement: he characteristically argues a delicate point by telling a story. Let me follow his lead.

Picture Wilde on the Fourteenth of February in 1895, backstage at the St. James Theatre in London. The habitual elegance of his appearance is considerably muted in the dim lights of the wings. Indeed, his appearance had sobered of late: at just about that time when his plays began to succeed he gave up the velvet knee breeches which had been his sartorial signature during early adulthood. (Ada Leverson speaks of his having been dressed that evening with "a sort of florid sobriety.") But more than darkness and a *slight* swerve towards more conservative tailoring restrain the air of carefree ease that makes him seem, in his photographs, like so much human drapery. I hope I shall not be betraying probability by making the irreverent suggestion that Wilde is *concentrating* backstage at the St. James. Franklin Dyall, who played Merriman in the first production, provides the evidence here. His role had rather few lines, but one of them won him the loudest and most sustained laugh of his career. The line was, "Mr. Ernest Worthing has just driven over from the station. He has brought his luggage with him," and it is Wilde's response to the laugh that proves how closely he was attending to the performance: Dyall reports, "As I came off Wilde said to me: 'I'm so glad you got that laugh. It shows they have followed the plot.' "

Let me explain why I think the anecdote is important. I shall try to obey Wilde's alter ego, Algernon Montcrieff, who tells his friend Jack, "Now produce your explanation, and pray make it improbable." The plot.

Let me tell you a plot. It begins, if you will excuse the formulation, years after it begins. What I mean to say is that the events of this play involve a complicated investigation of how things got into the state of confusion in which we find the characters at the beginning of the play itself. Years earlier an infant had been separated from its parents, an unfortunate fact of biography that has hardly inhibited the baby from growing up to be a hero and from getting a play named after him. Through a complex chain of events he discovers his true identity and is reunited with his family. It all leads up to a spectacular final scene, perhaps the most famous scene in the history of Western drama. Indeed it is probably the most famous play in the history of Western drama. It is called *Oedipus Rex*.

I trust that it will be granted that the comparison of Wilde's play to Sophocles' is sufficiently improbable. Certainly the plots are not *absolutely* identical. Wilde has taken considerable care about this. In the Greek story, for example, the hero has a terrifying encounter with a she-dragon famous for asking difficult questions and I want to insist that it would be entirely inappropriate to compare the sphinx to Lady Bracknell, who is, as Jack puts it, "a monster without being a myth." But there's no denying that Wilde flirts brilliantly with *Oedipus Rex,* elements of which drop casually and hilariously into *The Importance of Being Earnest.* Sophocles' story is essentially about mistaking one's relatives, of confusing mother and wife, and Wilde toys with such confusion in a wonderfully sidelong manner during the first act when he has Algernon muse, in mock perplexity, over "why an aunt, should call her own nephew her uncle." Certainly the central irony of Sophocles' play is that the bed of conception and birth should be transformed into a bier, a site of death. Ancient as this paradox is, it is news to the monstrous Lady Bracknell, who insists that "Until yesterday I had no idea that there were any families or persons whose origin was a Terminus."

Lady B is punning, of course, and that is just the point: Wilde is steadily converting the tragic into the comic, ironic paradox into shrewd witticism. That is an old strategy, of course: Roman New Comedy took just this sort of tragic or romance plot—of foundlings, confusions of identity, and scrambled erotic attachment—and made it its own, asserting equal rights to such confusions. If it weren't for its dalliance with the plot of *Oedipus Rex,* it might be enough to speak of Wilde's play simply as another New Comedy. Perhaps it would be truer to say that *The Importance of Being Earnest* recovers the originary moment of New Comedy, and renews it.

My improbable explanation has a number of implications which I want to tease out a bit. The first is that it might help to focus our attention on the play more appropriately. It has become the custom for inattentive directors to concentrate, in casting, on Algernon and Lady Bracknell, and then to let the rest of the roles get sorted out as best they can. But if *The Importance of Being Earnest* is indeed a comic imitation of *Oedipus Rex,* then it is clearly Jack, or Ernest, as he in fact discovers himself to be, who is at the dramatic center. It is he, after all, who turns out to possess the crucial name—you will notice that at the end of the play Wilde finesses the problem that Algernon *can't* take the name of Ernest, for his long-lost brother has title to that title, which leaves Algy stuck as Algy (and, as Cecily has said before, she might not be able to give a person so named her "undivided attention"). At any rate, it is more important to be Jack than Algernon, since Jack is Ernest, and thus is the elder brother, the true heir to the Montcrieff fortune, and above all, the possessor of the magic name. But he is important for other reasons as well.

It is often objected that Wilde's characters all talk more or less alike, that the characters are all more or less the same. But Jack Worthing does not talk like Algernon Montcrieff. He aspires to talk like Algernon, aspires to the masterful urbanity of an Algernon, but he is a dreadful failure at it. He loses his cigarette case, gets stuck with the bill for dinner, fails to get more than a muffin or two of his own to eat in the third act and a few portions of bread and butter in the first, while Algernon gorges on the cucumber sandwiches and gets almost all of the muffins. The fact is that Jack is too much in earnest. His deceptions are in service of the most formal and pedestrian courtship, whereas Algernon deceives in order to flirt wildly.

Before the trip to Jack's place in Hertfordshire, Algernon's deceptions had always been in service of nothing but deception itself. Both deception and flirtation have the same name for Algy; both are called "Bunburying." This is Important. For Algy, artifice and eros have the same name, whereas for Ernest, they are opposed. As with Buster Keaton, the elegance of Jack's facade is constantly being betrayed by the earnestness within. In Wilde, as in Keaton's best films, concentration is a kind of distraction. The huge difference between Algernon and Jack is nowhere more obvious than at their entrances in act 2. When Jack appears, he looks like an undertaker; when Algernon enters, he looks like an ad for Christian Dior.

And of course *that* is why the play's curtain line is so very good. When Jack says, "I've now realized for the first time in my life the vital Importance of Being Earnest" he is punning, like Lady Bracknell talking about origins and terminuses. What he means is that it's important to have the name, Ernest, and that that's the only "Earnest-ness" that's good for anything at all. Seriousness hasn't done him any good in the course of the play; worst of all, seriousness has sapped all of his deceptions of fluency, of artistry. The last line is a sign that Jack has finally learned his lesson, which is that he must stop caring so much about things, stop trying to keep up appearances for Cecily's sake. Appearances must be kept up, says Wilde, for their *own* sake, because appearances are so very nice to look at.

So that is the first implication of the link between this play and *Oedipus Rex:* both plays, like most good plays, dramatize the hero's coming-to-knowledge, in this case a coming-to-knowledge about the use and abuse of seriousness that frees the characters to get down to some genuine artificiality. The next implication has to do with the very fact that comparing the two plays seems so improbable. In Sophocles' play, plot is nearly everything, whereas in Wilde's play, the plot has a tendency to disappear under the wonderful surface of aphorism. I could again quote the play to illustrate my point about the value of plotting: take the little exchange between Algernon and Jack at the end of act 1, where Jack objects to Algernon's delightfully complicated techniques for pitching woo. "If you don't take care," he says, "your friend Bunbury will get you into a serious scrape one of these days," to which Algernon replies, "I love scrapes. They are the only things that are never serious." Scrapes is a handy term, since it trivializes those contortions of strategem and coincidence which are at the center of Sophoclean plotting. When Algernon says that such plotting, such scrapes, are never serious, he is speaking as Wilde the literary critic. And here a bit of dramatic history will be useful.

William Archer, the critic to whom I referred earlier, was not only a fan of Wilde's, he was the chief spokesman for a movement in English dramatic writing that was advocating a new attention to social issues and that would find an idiom which would lend philosophical and tragic dignity to matters of political and topical concern. What Archer was in fact reacting to was the pervasive influence of the dramatic techniques of the French playwright Eugène Scribe, the master of the so-called "Well-Made Play." The well-made play is characterized by precisely that calculation of scheme and coincidence, that trick of falling into place, which is the signal feature of *Oedipus Rex.* Now Wilde's attitude to both the old school of Scribe and the new school of Archer is subtle and hilarious. In effect he accepts Archer's position that the well-made play is a kind of dramatic Bunburying, nothing but a sequence of "scrapes," but then he fails to join Archer in a full-scale assault on such plotting. What Wilde is doing, if you will permit a slight anachronism, is to make the well-made play into a kind of "camp." No wonder Archer felt perplexed by Wilde. Wilde was lavishing a mock literary nostalgia on Scribe, but without identifying himself with the forces of what

Archer regarded as "progressive" playwrighting. Archer is the theatrical spokesman for a particular kind of Victorian value, what Matthew Arnold called "high seriousness," compounded with a degree of reformist fervor; Wilde called it "earnestness" and punned it out of existence.

It's an extremely powerful effect. First of all, Wilde manages to absorb Scribe's techniques by imitating Scribe's great Sophoclean model, but—as I said before—he inundates this plot with a tide of wonderfully musical wit, so that you hardly notice the plot which provides the technical underpinnings of the drama. Scribe and Sophocles endure an homage that leaves them looking rather frail and silly. And when we get to that very stagey last line, which is right out of Scribe, and miles beneath the literary standards of Archer's favorite playwrights, we hardly notice that the line really is summing up the play, really is showing us how irrelevant Arnoldian or Archerian seriousness is to the world of Wilde's plays. All of Wilde's influences come out looking sheepish at best.

Archer against Scribe, Scribe against Archer. Nowhere does the trick of getting one's predecessors to beat each other into jelly show up so powerfully as it does during the final scene of the play. As we are discovering the secret of Jack's mysteriously terminal origins, a fine sequence of exchanges take place. Jack announces his identity to Miss Prism and Wilde signals the particularly conventional quality of the scene by telling us that the lines are delivered "in a pathetic voice." Here is the exchange:

> JACK: Miss Prism, more is restored to you than this handbag.
> I was the baby you placed in it.
> MISS PRISM (*amazed*): You?
> JACK (*embracing her*): Yes . . . mother!

This out-Scribes Scribe. More is falling into place than actually needs to fall into place, for Miss Prism is *not* Jack's mother. But it takes several more lines in order to straighten the misunderstanding out. Miss Prism responds, "recoiling in indignant astonishment" according to the stage direction:

> MISS PRISM: Mr. Worthing! I am unmarried!
> JACK: Unmarried! I do not deny that is a serious blow. But
> after all, who has the right to cast a stone against one
> who has suffered? Why should there be one law for men,
> and another for women? Mother, I forgive you!

Since the fate of the fallen woman is one of the great staples of late Victorian social drama in the Archer tradition, what we have here is a perfect example of out-Archering Archer. The breadth of spirit, the exquisite liberality of young Ernest Worthing is utterly unnecessary here, so that Scribe's plotting has disabled Archer's principles. It is a cunning scene, and a cunning piece of dramatic criticism.

Wilde's other plays are not really very good, but noticing the way in which they fail may help us to understand the peculiar character of Wilde's success in *Earnest*. Of all Wilde's other plays, the one that comes closest to working is his serious attempt to write an Archerian fallen woman play, *Lady Windermere's Fan*. (Archerian in conception, but *also* neatly Scribal: the crucial fan—like the handbag at Victoria Station—is an object invested with remarkable power over plot; such potent props were a staple of Scribe's well-made play.) It fails because Wilde can't get his tone to settle down enough to accommodate the plot. Instead, the dialogue frequently rallies itself up to a sparkle that gets in the way of the slow workings of suspicion and self-defense that knit the play together. Wilde was shrewd enough to recognize finally that he didn't really like plots, so when he sat down to write *Earnest* he took a few bits of the most famous plot in existence, crumpled them up, and then smothered them with mannerism: in effect, he adapts form to content by papering over the content. That he chooses what must be called the master-plot of Western drama is both characteristically sophomoric and characteristically self-aware: if one is uncomfortable with plotting, why not sabotage the model of plotting, so that plotting itself will look like a game not worth playing?

The gesture is less cavalier than perhaps I have made it seem. If Wilde sacrifices plot to the surface sparkle of aphorism it's because he is one of the great English philosophers of the surface. It is also because he is, in his own way, a *moralist* of the surface.

The best way to explain what I mean by this is to change the subject. Consider a passage by another great poetic moralist, a passage from *The Marriage of Heaven and Hell* in which Blake gives his own very special definitions for the two partners, Heaven and Hell, whose marriage he is announcing:

> Without Contraries is no progression. Attraction and Repulsion, Reason and Energy, Love and Hate, are necessary to Human existence.
>
> From these contraries spring what the religious call Good & Evil. Good is the passive that obeys Reason. Evil is the active springing from Energy.

In what seems a moment of rhetorical condensation, Blake finishes his definitions thus:

> Good is Heaven, Evil is Hell.

Now this is very shrewd. The definitions stack up in such a way that one begins to suspect that Good is not so good, and that Evil, if it's allied to energy and activity, can't be all bad. So when we get to the final line it's hard to know how to take it. Yet it has the outward form of a perfectly comprehensible, perfectly orthodox assertion: Heaven is the good place, hell the bad place. Not only do we not know how to take it when Blake says this, not only do we not know what he means by heaven, if it's good and good is passive and cut off from energy, but we also begin to doubt the very form of such pronouncements. What Blake manages to do is to take the form of the aphorism and make us wonder why we usually have such an unquestioning and docile attitude to ideas when they're cut up for us so neatly. The very simplicity of the proverb form is on display, and under attack.

Wilde may well owe as much to Blake as did his young friend Yeats. Certainly Wilde is no more devoted to witty iconoclasm than is Blake; certainly Wilde is no less devoted a practitioner of the anti-authoritarian proverb than is Blake. Blake's defense of the imaginary over the merely factual, as in the line, "What is now proved was once merely imagined," could be a snatch from Wilde's conversation, while Wilde's "Even things that are true can be proved" sounds just like Blake. (Only such an embittered remark as Wilde's "A thing isn't necessarily true because a man dies for it" reveals something—specifically a bitter hostility to romantic idealism—that could legitimately be claimed as beyond Blake's reach.) Both men are primarily interested in the Witticism as a form, because it manages to disguise the rebellious in the very garb of the prescriptive.

Consider the opening witticism from Wilde's famous "Phrases and Philosophies for the Young":

> The first duty in life is to be as artificial as possible. What the
> second duty is no one has as yet discovered.

Part of what makes this brilliant is that it seems to promise that you could make a list, in descending order of importance, of what a person ought to do. It then quite splendidly fails to deliver on the promise. At the same moment that it lays down a law, it makes a monkey of lawyers, who can't remember all the commandments but are sure that there are ten of them. The lawyers knew that they were being made monkeys of, though, for when Wilde was on trial for his relations with Douglas, the lawyers interrogated him very closely on "Phrases and Philosophies for the Young," recognizing that the form of the witty phrase itself was under attack, that the notion that morality can be summarized, that its complexities can be distilled into Rules was crumbling under Wilde's gloved hand.

Besides its crucial function of obscuring the plot, how does the form of witticism operate in *The Importance of Being Earnest*? Again, Wilde gives the characters something very telling to say on the matter. Here, again, is Algernon:

> ALGERNON: All women become like their mothers. That
>   is their tragedy. No man does. That's his.
> JACK: Is that clever?
> ALGERNON: It is perfectly phrased! and quite as true as any
>   observation in civilized life should be.

Algernon is telling us exactly how to take the play. We are to approve the elegance of its phrasing, and to take its claims to truth with strictly measured amounts of salt. The witticism does not pretend to truth with a capital T. What it pretends to is *accuracy,* by which I mean to say something like occasional appropriateness to the sweet and petty business of getting along in polite society, an observation pertinent, not to reality, but to civilized life.

It should be clear now why I intended to entitle this piece "Wilde as Moralist." Like Blake, Wilde hated Truths. They hated them because Truths put blinders on us, tell us what to do before we know who we are or where we are, in whose company, in what room. The primary function of Wilde's witticisms, so neatly packaged and so perfectly balanced, is to erode our confidence in neat packaging and perfect balance as a vehicle for inculcating ethical values. Wilde's description of a cigarette might as well be a description of the witticism as a form, or of *Earnest* as a piece of dramatic construction; "A cigarette," he says, "is the perfect type of a perfect pleasure. It is exquisite, and it leaves one unsatisfied." The witticism excites our delight in matters of moral concern and steadily denies us the satisfaction of easy or universally adequate reflections on those matters.

This, I take it, is a moral position. To bury plot under clever talk is to insist that what happens to people is never as important as what people make of what happens to them. Each time an event sinks beneath a wave of wit we are being shown how much more valuable sense is than sensation. And when a second witticism shoulders aside a first, and a third displaces the second, we are being shown that any act of making sense of sensation is merely provisional. Wilde shows us that there are no satisfactory rules to lay down about life save that no matter what happens, it is always pleasant to lay down a rule about it; or to translate this in such a way that it reveals the moral passion that animated so much of Wilde's work: There are no Moral Laws; there is only moral labor. Hence the justice of what Borges has to say about the man: "Like Gibbon, like Johnson, like Voltaire, he was an ingenious man who was also right."

Idyll of the Marketplace

Regenia Gagnier

Beatrice Webb wrote that in the 1890's London Society included a mixed bag representing the governing class. With the Court, Cabinet and ex-Cabinet, financiers, and "the racing set," she included the better known artists and reviewers who habitually entertained these groups. Because *A Woman of No Importance* followed Wilde's first major success, *Lady Windermere's Fan,* it drew the sort of crowd (in the sort of attire) that kept Society columnists scribbling for months. Max Beerbohm wrote that "all the politicians were there." The first-night audience included "the arts, literature, law, and politics" (*Stage,* 20 April 1893) and, we might add, science. Beerbohm named the elements of the spectacular Society: Arthur Balfour, Joseph Chamberlain, Lord Battersea, the Randolph Churchills, Sir Edward Clarke, Shaw-Lefevre, Baron de Rothschild, Lord Wolverton, Henry Wyndham, George Lewis, Sir Spenser Wells, Burne-Jones, Conan Doyle, Richard Le Gallienne; and "Henry Rochefort stood for France." The Prince of Wales attended a few nights later, and the costume on stage and off filled the women's columns in subsequent weeks. The reviews indicate that the grandeur of the audience was to be matched in theater history only by that of the audience at *The Importance of Being Earnest.*

Florence Alexander described the opulent but *intime* atmosphere of those first nights as "great events," the technical arrangement of which she supervised personally, "sick with anxiety," down to the color-coordinating

From *Idylls of the Marketplace: Oscar Wilde and the Victorian Public.* © 1986 by the Board of Trustees of the Leland Stanford Junior University. Stanford University Press, 1986.

109

of set and costume and the arranging of flowers: "Our firstnights . . . were like brilliant parties. Everybody knew everybody, everybody put on their best clothes, everybody wished us success." In *The Plays of Oscar Wilde,* Alan Bird describes the mirror of their own luxury that such audiences saw in Wilde's comedies, and the identification that public figures like the Prince Regent and his mistresses could feel with Wilde's characters. Of the intimacy that the host Mrs. Alexander recalled, Bird writes: "The rapport between management and all sections of the audience also extended to the actors and to the playwrights. . . . Wilde was able to play the parts of host and master magician at the same time. . . . His appearance on the stage, at the end of the play, with a cigarette in his hand, was perfectly appropriate: he was in his own drawing-room, a situation only possible in the reformed and renovated theatres of the 1890's." As recently as 1976, Martin Green associated this image of an exclusive Society and its trappings with Wilde's comedies when he wrote that for him entering Cambridge on a Butler Scholarship "was to feel every nerve of self-consciousness as unwelcomely stimulated as if I'd walked on to a stage set for *Lady Windermere's Fan.*"

If Wilde turned the theater into a drawing room, his plays turned the audience into consumers. The plays worked like fetishes for members of the audience who identified with Society. They followed the characters in imputing to artificial objects or imaginary constructs strange properties. These properties consisted in the objects' or constructs' imputed ability to fulfill wishes. In "The Decay of Lying," Wilde could see the West's fetishism of Eastern ways and peoples in British orientalism and *japonisme.* Because he was a typical Victorian poseur, he was well acquainted with what in "The Soul of Man under Socialism" he called "the things and symbols of things" to which people attached great value. In his plays, his understanding of fetishism was theatrical rather than theoretical. He supplied the one fetish for the audience that would distract it enough to allow his criticisms: an overvalued and exceedingly powerful image of itself. Since Brummell, this had been the dandies' stratagem: to stylize Society; to so refine that style personally as to put its bearers to shame; and then to be of two minds regarding that style and that Society. Wilde presented on a small scale what Debord calls the spectacle as a self-portrait of power, in which one part of the world represents itself to the world and is superior to it. It is allied to commodity fetishism and occurs, says Debord, "the moment when the commodity has attained the total occupation of social life." It is a presentation of a Society for whom all wishes come true.

The next generation, of [Antonin] Artaud and the Alfred Jarry Theater (1926–30), would theorize a critical spectacular drama as theater of cruelty.

. . . In "The Alchemical Theater" Artaud compared theater to alchemy: they were both virtual arts that did not carry their ends in themselves; far from being an auracular object of contemplation, the drama was to be "an intentional provocation" to its "double," the audience. In theater of cruelty the focus shifts from spectacle to spectator, from the production to consumption of the work.

In so formulating the drama, Artaud attempted to situate it in mass society. The referent of bourgeois art, or psychological realism, was the interiority of the few, and it fostered either an exclusive or a complacent relation with its audience; it was addressed to the understanding. This bourgeois privatization, Artaud felt, was obsolescent in a world of mass control and mass violence. The new theater offered undeceptive violence and was addressed to the only faculties not benumbed by the modern world: it would be a sensational drama, addressed to the senses. (To cure the soul with the senses, said Dorian Gray.) Similarly, *Earnest* is not addressed to the understanding but to the senses. It reflects, not violence, but the breakdown of human community through commodity fetishism.

Obviously, *The Conquest of Mexico*—as described in the Theater of Cruelty's "Second Manifesto," with its exposure of "the ever active fatuousness of Europe"—was intended to provoke the audience on a scale well beyond the modest goals of Wilde's society drama. Whereas Artaud wanted to display and provoke modern society into self-hatred or humiliation, Wilde simply displayed it, with a critique inherent in the play. Yet in its specific attacks on the consciences of middle-class audiences, the Alfred Jarry Theater of Cruelty barely did more than make explicit what Wilde had dramatized for Society and an aspiring bourgeoisie.

For example, in *Victor, or the Children Are in Power,* Artaud and Roger Vitrac practiced mental cruelty on middle-class audiences. In a 48-page brochure entitled *The Alfred Jarry Theater and Public Hostility* (1930), *Victor* was advertised as "a middle-class play in three acts by Roger Vitrac. This play, lyrical at times, ironic, even outspoken at others, was aimed at the middle-class family unit. It featured adultery, incest, scatology, anger, Surrealist poetry, patriotism, madness, shame and death." Unlike *The Importance of Being Earnest,* which also, as critics have recognized, satirizes every institution the British held sacred—family, politics, work, education, marriage, truth, colonialism, religion, friendship, feminine modesty, science, statistics, romantic love, and others—at the conclusion of *Victor,* a sort of comic version of the Little Father Time story in *Jude the Obscure,* the characters are not even left alive.

Wilde's theater used techniques similar to Artaud's, and the ways in which both fetishized the audience or public may be seen as a logical product of mass consumerist society; their statements and manifestos parody the advertiser's cynical inclusion of the public. In making the audience "an integral part of our efforts" (1926 Manifesto), Artaud extended the "stage" to include the entire auditorium. He described the mise-en-scène as "the visual and plastic materialization of speech, the language of everything that can be said and signified upon a stage independently of speech, everything that finds its expression in space, or that can be affected or disintegrated by it" ("The Oriental and Occidental Theater"). In *Earnest* the stage was a continuation of the audience; but, again as in Artaud, the actors/characters were not.

Artaud felt that traditional sympathetic identification lulled the senses of the spectator, so he rehearsed his actors in de-identification, or ultra-stylized, jerky, and exaggerated moves, stripping the action of any naturalism. As Victor Corti put it [in his introduction to Artaud's works], "all theater's traditional and well-loved tricks were amplified (sometimes coming dangerously close to parody) until stage illusion was shattered, the reality of the plays then standing out as naked as those puppets which featured in its productions." This exactly describes the unnaturalism of *Earnest*. Artaud's gigantic puppets were, like the name of his theater, adapted from a play almost exactly contemporary with Wilde's, Alfred Jarry's *Ubu Roi* (1896), whose stage illusion also shattered to expose what Cyril Connolly saw as a prophecy, "the Santa Claus of the Atomic Age." Wilde was allied to Jarry through more than mutual friends and directors like Lugné-Poe, who produced *Salome*. His audience identified with the spectacle, de-identified with the characters, and called his actors "puppets." His theater parodied theater and thus revealed the reality of the plays.

The Importance of Being Earnest operates on three levels: the superiority of author to audience, the mutuality of audience and stage image (mimesis, or mise-en-scène in Artaud's sense), and the audience's superiority to the farce. The material images on stage are a direct mimesis of the audience, its mirror image: an idle, luxuried community in an opulent environment of props and costumes. The play's dialogue, however, includes the author's trenchant criticisms of the audience; on this level, the author is greater than the audience. The lowest level consists of farcical action, an indication of the author's lunacy, and this has the effect of canceling the author's superior status as a critic. The absurdity of the action allows the audience to label it farce, implying that its marvelous triviality has the sole purpose of inciting laughter, while the audience simultaneously extricates itself from the charges leveled against it. If the author is critical of the audience, his play's absurd action permits the audience to be superior to him. While the social criticism and farcical action effectively cancel each other out, the audience receives reinforcement from its own dominant and fetishized image on stage.

This dominant image includes another mimetic aspect, and this was the source of the play's overwhelming success: the representation of the Society for whom all wishes come true. The audience at the St. James's could make fetishes real, could spin straw into gold. Wilde exploited this representation for his own gain, even while he criticized it.

The first two acts of *Earnest* (a play in which even the punning title raises the issue of the presence or absence of the mythical "earnestness") elaborate the poses and objects by means of which the satirized upper classes fulfill their wishes. These are: the sick brother Ernest, who allows Jack to escape from his severe moral position as guardian in the country to life as a dandy in London; the invalid Bunbury, who allows Algy to escape dining with relatives (or, as Wilde elsewhere called relatives, "merely an exaggerated form of the public"); Jack's "romantic origin" in a handbag, which stirs "the deep fibres" of Gwendolen's nature; the name of "Ernest," which represents an ideal Gwendolen and Cecily have vowed to marry (when they learn that neither of their fiancés possesses the name, they break off the engagements); the young women's diaries, in which they write only imaginary events ("I never travel without my diary," says Gwendolen; "one should always have something sensational to read in the train"); and the fetish of Miss Prism's manuscript, which is perhaps the most brilliant in the play. These theatrical devices are either fetishized poses or fetishized things and ideals, whose phantasmic properties command practical results.

Miss Prism, as the play indicates, is sexually forlorn. Like her counterpart, the Reverend Canon Chasuble, D.D., the only way her sexuality surfaces is in metaphor, a release unnecessary for the other characters in the play, whose power, presumably, permits them more accessible outlets. CHASUBLE: "Were I fortunate enough to be Miss Prism's pupil, I would hang upon her lips. (MISS PRISM *glares*.) I spoke metaphorically.—My metaphor was drawn from bees." MISS PRISM: "Maturity can always be depended on. Ripeness can be trusted. Young women are green. (DR CHASUBLE *starts*.) I spoke horticulturally. My metaphor was drawn from fruits." Similarly, the gaps in Miss Prism's life are revealed with comic pathos in her excessive affection for her personified handbag:

> It seems to be mine. Yes, here is the injury it received through the upsetting of a Gower Street omnibus in younger and happier

days. Here is the stain on the lining caused by the explosion of
a temperance beverage, an incident that occurred at Leamington.
And here, on the lock, are my initials. I had forgotten that in
an extravagant mood I had them placed there. The bag is un-
doubtedly mine. I am delighted to have it restored to me. It has
been a great inconvenience being without it all these years.

When it turns out that this poor woman had placed her manuscript in the
pram and the baby in her handbag, we have a brilliant parody of the
fetishism of manuscript-as-child of a frustrated parent that Ibsen had treated
much more seriously in *Hedda Gabler.*

But where other writers, such as Ibsen, George Eliot, and Dickens,
had shown the pathos and futility of fetishes, generally because within the
classes they wrote about the fetishized objects were associated with dreams
incapable of fulfillment, Wilde treats the effectiveness of fetishes among the
upper classes. In fact, the characters in this play care little about actual
material, for the appearance of material is quite enough to get by: "Algernon
is an extremely, I may almost say an ostentatiously, eligible young man.
He has nothing, but he looks everything. What more can one desire?" In
the original four-act version, when Algernon is "attached" for an outstand-
ing bill of £762 for eating at the Savoy, he responds to the solicitor: "Pay
it? How on earth am I going to do that? You don't suppose I have got any
money? How perfectly silly you are. No gentleman ever has any money."
In *Earnest,* indeed, the fetishes materialize as "truth." Jack becomes Ernest,
and acquires a real brother in Algy; Gwendolen marries her Ernest; Cecily's
fiction in her diary materializes as a real engagement to Algernon; Miss
Prism and Dr. Chasuble, whose "unpublished sermons" make him the
perfect mate for the woman who has "lost" or "mislaid" her manuscript
as she had lost or mislaid the baby, embrace at the end; and Lady Bracknell,
who had always fetishized family, is quite satisfied with the revelation of
the orphan Jack as her "natural" nephew.

It was because Wilde had so accurately assessed the exclusive value of
appearances for his audience that Shaw found the play heartless and un-
moving, and that other middle-class critics found it trivial (meaning superficial). Contrary to the practice of psychological realism, Wilde seemed
to say that internality, depth of character, and bonds of human affection
were negligible in the society represented by *Earnest,* a society of spectacle
only. All that mattered was the authority of the participants' poses and the
glitter of their props. "Our social relations had no roots in neighborhood,
in vocation, in creed, or for that matter in race," Webb wrote of Society

in the 1890s, "they likened a series of moving pictures—surface impressions without depth—restlessly stimulating in their variety." Even the fast, epigrammatic language of *Earnest* functions perfectly as a political tool, which, if handled properly, can manipulate others and establish one in the highest social spheres. But beyond its political force, it is a language in which it is impossible to communicate in earnest.

The characters in *Earnest* assume *all* knowledge, not only truisms but the inverse of truisms. When they invert a Victorian platitude for their own ends, they not only state the opposite of what the audience expects but they include by inference the opposite of their own inversion. Such a discourse leaves no room for interference or input from others. The expected lines are assumed in the unexpected, and their interplay is self-generating, precluding all interference from the outside, that is, from other speakers: a closed system representing an exclusive society. Wilde himself had used this verbal technique to dominate drawing rooms. It amounts to the reification of the insurrectionary style of diversion . . . and it appears today in the work of some postmodern architects. A wit subverting sincerity can be liberating and dialectical. A whole society of wits, as in *Earnest,* renders insincerity static, a mere tool of personal power in service of the status quo. Wit, in this case, is entirely subservient to a traditional plot of marriage and money exchange.

Limited to platitudes and their inversions, the characters operate within frames of reference as static as their power is seemingly unshakable. As Barbey had written in *Of Dandyism and of George Brummell,* the "tradition" of the British upper classes was stultifying. Wild's images of them at tea or in the garden are of mannequins fixed in their masks. Their chins, says Lady Bracknell, are "worn very high." They do no work, their play is stylized, and the comedy concludes with a "tableau" (a static image) of traditional comic marriages—perhaps the most stultifying of all bourgeois institutions. At the end of *Salome,* Herod represents a fallen image of such a stultified ruling class. As Wilde had deplored the "things and symbols of things" that fixed the parameters of upper-class life for the restrictions they imposed on their possessors, so the impotent Herod concludes that "it is not wise to find symbols in everything that one sees," and he retires to his mirror where he sees only a "mask."

Since power to some extent depends on the maintenance and conservation of its symbols, the poses and fetishes in *Earnest* symbolize power even while their static representation is inherently conservative and prevents progress. As there could be no development but the repetition of clichéd forms in *Earnest,* Wilde felt that there could be no progress for the powerful ruling classes. Even if his audience had suspected this interpretation, it would have remained undisturbed, for it was content where it was. Furthermore, the newly "arrived" in that audience could identify with images of the aristocracy they had successfully supplanted. While the 1890s gave rise to consolidated reaction against all major labor unions, including the Engineers', Miners', Dockers', and Seamen's, and Woodworkers', Wilde's conservative images and his characters' witty disparagement of the lower classes (who were not present in the theater) served as positive reinforcement of the maintenance of the old way.

If this power illustrated by preemptory speech leaves no room for progress or development, it also leaves no room for internal life and individuated character. The characters' wishes consist in the reinforcement of their poses. "What wonderfully blue eyes you have," Gwendolen informs Jack, "They are quite, quite blue. I hope you will always look at me just like that, especially when there are other people present." Cecily's diary, as its owner instructs her fiancé, "is simply a very young girl's record of her own thoughts and impressions, and consequently meant for publication. When it appears in volume form I hope you will order a copy." The needs of Wilde's characters are conditioned by the status quo. Jack desires to know the identity of his parents, not for psychological reasons, but rather because Society requires that it be known. Whereas for everybody the name of Ernest is extremely important for its portentous sound, the fact that it was the name of Algy's father is so insignificant that Algy has forgotten it. This is a more radical critique of a mass mentality than even Artaud's, for Artaud still exploited internality sufficiently to describe Vitrac's *Secrets of Love* as "an ironic play, physically staging the misgivings, dual isolation, eroticism and criminal thoughts lurking in the minds of lovers" ("The Alfred Jarry Theater and Public Hostility").

Twentieth-century critics have imputed to the social poses of Bunburying a map of Wilde's alleged guilt for his own "double life." The inspiration of Bunburying may well have derived from Wilde's homosexual experience; certainly the subplot of the original version, in which Algy faces imprisonment in Holloway for debts at the Savoy and Willis's, was a self-parody of Wilde's notorious extravagance. ("Well," says Algy, "I really am not going to be imprisoned in the suburbs for having dined in the West End.") Yet *Earnest* itself represents an arena in which poses are the norm. Wilde had earned his position in a similar arena by wearing clothes that even he thought were ridiculous, sending poems to Gladstone, dedicating them to women of Society, camping on Mrs. Langtry's doorstep, performing as was expected of him at an exhausting number of homes and clubs of the affluent, and in general learning which poses would help him and which would not. If he felt guilty, it certainly was not when he bragged that he had a play "written by a butterfly for butterflies."

As we might expect from the journalistic response to *Dorian Gray*, the very personal interaction between Wilde and his elite audience elicited more attacks on the author's presumptuousness. ("Mr. Wilde," a disgruntled reviewer of *A Woman of No Importance* had written in *Hearth and Home*, "is perhaps the most popular *middle-class* wit at present before the public" [5 April 1893, my italics].) This brings us to the other audience, those whom Wells called "the serious people who populate London." In *Earnest*, Wilde altogether eliminated representations of the lower classes, except, as was typical of his comedies, in the epigrams, where they were the subject of amusing commentary. The play was written for the kind of audience that frequented the St. James's. This apparent partiality for an elite audience won the contempt of the gentlemen of the press, who spoke for the serious people who populated London. The *Times*'s reviewer called the play a farce, the first vehicle sufficiently trivial for Wilde's epigrammatic style (15 February 1895). The *Athenaeum* criticized Wilde's "sheer wantonness of contempt for his public" in presenting a play with "not a gleam of sense or sanity" (23 February 1895). *Punch*, the monolith of middle-class humor, published a bogus interview with Wilde, "The O. W. Vade Mecum," which implied that the public who would follow him was beneath contempt (23 February 1895). Even Shaw, who had admired Wilde's earlier comedies, found *Earnest*, his most successful, old-fashioned in style and heartless in content. "Unless comedy touches me as well as amuses me," Shaw wrote in the *Saturday Review*, "it leaves me with a sense of having wasted my evening" (12 January 1895).

Although the upper-class audience responded wildly to *Earnest* and the middle-class journalists frowned, nonetheless—as Wells said—the play satirized the upper classes in a way that the critics might have approved. It contains the same acute social criticism that pervaded Wilde's earlier work. The upper-class characters speak epigrams exposing their own faults through ironic assertion or comic inversion. Incurably imperturbable and unselfconscious, they dominate the world by tone alone. For example, here is Gwendolen on upper-class idealism: "We live, as I hope you know, Mr. Worthing, in an age of ideals. The fact is constantly mentioned in the more expensive monthly magazines, and has reached the provincial pulpits, I am told; and my ideal has always been to love someone of the name of Ernest." Lady Bracknell on education: "Fortunately in England, at any rate, education produces no effect whatsoever. If it did, it would prove a serious danger to the upper classes, and probably lead to acts of violence in Grosvenor Square." Lady Bracknell on paternity: "To be born, or at any rate bred, in a hand-bag, whether it had handles or not, seems to me to display a contempt for the ordinary decencies of family life that reminds one of the worst excesses of the French Revolution. And I presume you know what that unfortunate movement led to?" Miss Prism on imperialism: "Cecily, you will read your Political Economy in my absence. The chapter on the Fall of the Rupee you may omit. It is somewhat too sensational." The original four-act version has an exchange between Cecily and Dr. Chasuble on economics. "I suppose you know all about the relations between Capital and Labour?" Cecily responds, "All I know about is the relations between Capital and Idleness—and that is merely from observation." And Lady Bracknell discusses thought (quite pointedly, since the statement reflects on all the preceding nonsense of the play): "Her unhappy father is, I am glad to say, under the impression that she is attending a more than usually lengthy lecture by the University Extension Scheme on the Influence of a permanent income on Thought."

The reviews of *Victor* that Artaud quotes in "The Alfred Jarry Theater and Public Hostility" could equally apply to *Earnest*: it dissected "all our existing institutions as well as the present state of middle-class society"; it was "a criticism of middle-class life and everything which is ridiculous and stupid about it: Society, the family, the Republic, the Army." In allowing Society to be reinforced by its own spectacle, however, Wilde exploited the society he criticized.

The Soul of Man under Victoria:
Iolanthe, The Importance of Being Earnest, and Bourgeois Drama

Susan Laity

> *"The mantle of Mr Gilbert has fallen on the shoulders of Mr Oscar Wilde,*
> *who wears it in the jauntiest fashion."*
>
> 1895 review of *The Importance of Being Earnest*

A trivial game for serious people might require the players to match unidentified quotations from the plays of Oscar Wilde and W. S. Gilbert with the right author. Some of the lines might be the following:

> Your Majesty says, "Kill a gentleman," and a gentleman is told off to be killed. Consequently, that gentleman is as good as dead—practically, he *is* dead—and if he is dead, why not say so?

> "The doctors found out that Bunbury could not live . . . so Bunbury died." "He seems to have had great confidence in the opinion of his physicians."

> "This gentleman is seen,
>   With a maid of seventeen;
> A-taking of his *dolce far niente;*
>   And wonders he'd achieve,
>   For he asks us to believe
> She's his mother—and he's nearly five-and-twenty."

> "Recollect yourself, I pray,
> And be careful what you say—
>
> . . . .
>
> For I really do not see
> How so young a girl could be
> The mother of a man of five-and-twenty."

But why does your aunt call you her uncle? "From little Cecily, with her fondest love to her dear Uncle Jack." There is no objection, I admit, to an aunt being a small aunt, but why an aunt, no matter what her size may be, should call her own nephew her uncle, I can't quite make out.

I don't want to say a word against brains—I've a great respect for brains—I often wish I had some myself—but with a House of Peers composed exclusively of people of intellect, what's to become of the House of Commons?

The whole theory of modern education is radically unsound. Fortunately in England, at any rate, education produces no effect whatsoever. If it did, it would prove a serious danger to the upper classes, and probably lead to acts of violence in Grosvenor Square.

"We won't wait long." "No. We might change our minds. We'll get married first." "And change our minds afterwards?" "That's the usual course."

"A man who marries without knowing Bunbury has a very tedious time of it." "That is nonsense. If I marry a charming girl . . . I certainly won't want to know Bunbury." "Then your wife will."

These passages were taken at random (well, practically at random) from Gilbert's *Mikado* and *Iolanthe* and from Wilde's *Importance of Being Earnest*. And their similarity of tone implies that Wilde has, in fact, assimilated Gilbert's language, donned his mantle. Should we, then, greet the author of *Earnest*, coming onstage to accept the acclaim of his enthusiastic first-night audience, with a pointed: "Mr. Gilbert, I presume?" This essay presumes to answer that question.

  Not all of the many critics who have seen the figure of Gilbert lurking behind the Wildean mask have considered the comparison flattering, either to Gilbert or Wilde. George Bernard Shaw, in his unfavorable review of *Earnest*, attributed its worst flaws to its "unfortunate moment of Gilbertism," to wit, the second-act dialogue between Cecily and Gwendolen, and to a Gilbertian heartlessness throughout. Lionel Trilling, in his introduction to the Oxford edition of *Earnest,* writes: "[The world of the play] is also, of course, the world of nonsense, that curious invention of the English of the nineteenth century, of Lewis Carroll and Edward Lear, and (although he is of a lower order) W. S. Gilbert, from whom Wilde borrowed to good effect: that baby in the suitcase is sheer Gilbert." Lynton Hudson's study in 1951, *The English Stage 1850–1950,* on the other hand, details the resemblances between *Earnest* and a not very successful comedy (only commercially—it is a splendid play) of Gilbert's, *Engaged* (1877), and concludes that *Earnest* may not, therefore, be considered an original play, however delightful. And at a conference celebrating the 150th anniversary of Gilbert's birth, a colleague told me that, had he received *Earnest* as a student paper, he would have had to fail it for plagiarism, again because of its similarity to *Engaged.* That Wilde, at least in *Earnest,* sounds Gilbertian is indisputable; that he may well have had scenes from the unjustly neglected *Engaged* in mind when he wrote *Earnest* is by no means proven, but perfectly possible. But that the aims of Wilde in *The Importance of Being Earnest* were the same as those of Gilbert in *Engaged* or, indeed, in any of the great Savoy operas seems to me utterly to miss the glory of the work of either dramatist. For Gilbert, the English gentleman, and Wilde, the Irish dandy, fire disturbingly similar epigrams with utterly opposed aims.

Gilbert's farcical comedies (*Engaged, Tom Cobb, Foggerty's Fairy,* etc.) and the Savoy operas (Gilbert and Sullivan libretti) base themselves firmly in Victorian middle-class drama, engaging directly (if not always obviously) with bourgeois dramatic themes, stereotypes, and obsessions. Subversions of middle-class ideals, they remain, like their author, invincibly bourgeois. *The Importance of Being Earnest* (the only Wilde play this essay will deal with, for it is unique in Wilde's canon) deliberately excludes the middle class (except in the persons of Miss Prism and Canon Chasuble), creating an aristocratic comedy of dandies. Although it satirizes the middle class, it is not, finally, concerned with it, being instead an exploration of the role of the individual in society and the role of society in the development of the individual. In this essay, I shall compare *Iolanthe* with *Earnest,* in part because it (misleadingly) purports to concern the aristocracy (*Earnest*'s subject as well), in part because it is Gilbert's dramatic masterpiece, as *Earnest* is Wilde's.

Iolanthe (1882) is an Arcadian fairy farce set in the palace of Westminster, peopled by three incongruous sets of characters: an Arcadian shepherd and shepherdess, a group of Shakespearean (cum Wagnerian) fairies, and the members of the House of Peers, led by the Lord Chancellor, the highest judicial functionary in England. Fairy farce has a long tradition in the nineteenth-century British theater (and, indeed, a different, but parallel tradition in the French *folie féerie*), but never before had anyone sent the fairies into Westminster, or the House of Peers off to fairyland. Gilbert did both and almost got away with it: Queen Victoria knighted Sullivan in May 1883, in consideration of his "serious" music, but never knighted Gilbert, who was capable of equally "serious" (and equally dull) drama.

Although hundreds of hack playwrights wrote fairy farces throughout the nineteenth century, the term, and the genre, really came into their own with the work in the thirties, forties, and early fifties of James Robinson Planché, who even coined a new word for them, "extravaganzas." A Planché fairy extravaganza usually consists of a fairy tale, from the works of Perrault or the Countess D'Aulnoy, lavishly set and costumed, with songs, "transformation scenes," and a delicate humor which relies on the juxtaposition of the fantastic and the mundane: it peoples fairy tales with men and women who speak the language and share the concerns of Victorian Britons. The tone of Planché's whole oeuvre is caught in this brief exchange from *Blue Beard:*

> ABOMÉLIQUE (Blue Beard): How do you like my castle,
>   madam, say?
> FLEURETTE (Bride #20): I find your castle, sir, the truth to tell,
>   Superb! enchanting! matchless!—pretty well!
>   (*aside*) I'm dazzled quite with all I round me view.
>   I wish his beard was not so very blue.
> ABOMÉLIQUE: Madam, you flatter me by your approval,
>   I trust you'll think no longer of removal,
>   But make yourself at home—my house, my grounds,
>   My servants, coaches, horses, hawks and hounds,
>   Are yours, if you will have their master too.
> FLEURETTE (*aside*): I really think his beard is not so blue.
> ABOMÉLIQUE: My wealth's enormous—I've rent roll clear
>   Of forty millions—I'm a potent peer!
>   Likely to die before you, a great point sure—
>   A youthful peeress, with a thumping jointure!
>   The king himself might at your feet then fall.
> FLEURETTE (*aside*): I'm quite convinced his beard's not blue at
>   all;
>   Besides, if he's so very much my slave,
>   He'd be polite enough, perhaps, to shave.

Planché's prime aim was to reform both the matter and the presentation of burlesque/farce. Perhaps as much as the work of any one man, his extravaganzas brought the middle classes to the theater. They almost deserted burlesque, however, during the fifties, sixties, and seventies, when the broad farceurs and punsters—H. J. Byron, F. C. Burnand, and the brothers Brough—turned fairy burlesque into an extended snigger with their manic and mangled plots, titillating transvestitism, and low comic "gagging." Gilbert, who subscribed to a testimonial edition of Planché's *Extravaganzas* and entitled his first parody operas *New and Original Extravaganzas,* was seen by many (including Planché himself) as the man who would once more bring "respectability" to the farce.

While farce and burlesque declined in the social scale, melodrama, that other staple of lower-class drama, moved into the West End in the revamped form of "domestic drama" and "domestic comedy," where, for the first time, it became a popular middle-class amusement. When Queen Victoria, England's first bourgeois ruler (in sensibility and taste, not birth), attended productions of *Pauline* in 1851 and *The Corsican Brothers* in 1852, she sparked a dramatic change in middle-class attitudes toward the theater. To the mid-Victorian bourgeois audience the terms "drama" and "comedy" were almost interchangeable. Basically, the popular fare of the middle-class theater consisted of a simple plot, peopled by simple folk. The rising lad, the ideal-sentimental heroine and (frequently) her lively, practical sister (for this is the era of the double heroine), the fallen woman, the quiet man of affairs—these are the new ideals: good, bourgeois, domestic or domesticated souls all. (The fallen woman may seem like an odd choice here, but she both began and ended the mid-Victorian period—frequently standing in for the practical soubrette in the double heroine combination—as someone to be pitied, and, if she both repented and suffered sufficiently, forgiven.)

The stress, both in drama and comedy, is on the domestic, the quiet, the pure, and the mercantile, and the plays evoked from the audience the laughter that is never far from tears. This drama codified the way the middle class looked at itself, despite social realities which denied its every impulse. It claimed that "true hearts are more than coronets / And simple faith than Norman blood," but the only way to prove it was to reward the true hearted ones with coronets (after which they passed the Norman blood on to their children). Its self-made heroes rose through diligent effort, honesty, and thrift ("I polished up that handle so carefullee," sings Gilbert's Sir Joseph Porter, K.C.B., a middle-class social climber, "that now I am the Ruler of the Queen's Navee"). Its heroines became goddesses of the hearth, guardians of the domestic morals of the family, and, by extension, of a nation. Obsolete by the mid fifties, these characters clung to the stage until the dramatic revolution of the late eighties and nineties. Tom Robertson enshrined popular attitudes in his wildly popular and influential "realistic" plays of the late sixties, such as *Caste* (the quintessential mid-Victorian domestic drama) and *Society*. Their "cup-and-saucer realism," as it was called, lay in their staging and their simple, understated language and acting.

Gilbert, who admired Robertson as a stage manager (and worked with him on *Fun* magazine), and who tried with, for the most part, unfortunate results to write Robertsonian comedies, found in mid-Victorian domestic drama the subject for his true art, as he found in the Planché extravaganza the form. Wilde, an Irish self-proclaimed "Professor of Aesthetics," came to Victorian drama from vastly different circumstances with the perspective of an outsider. In a way quite different from Gilbert, however, he attacked similar targets.

Iolanthe, then, finds its origins and impulses deep within middle-class popular drama. Here before us are the conventional double heroines, in somewhat unconventional guise. Iolanthe is the fallen woman: a fairy, she has married a mortal (FLETA: "Is it injudicious to marry a mortal?" LEILA: "Injudicious? It strikes at the root of the whole fairy system!"). Her self-sacrifice, demonstrated initially by her courage in living "among the frogs" to be near her son and later by her willingness to face death so that Strephon may marry Phyllis, shows her repentance and worth. Phyllis is the simple country lass who knows that "in lowly cot / Alone is virtue found." She is the romantic, sentimental heroine of the play.

Iolanthe features the "blocking agent," as well, the overbearing matriarch, the Fairy Queen, who begins by stating the laws of the society but ends by being converted by the virtue of honest emotion. (When the fairies all become "fairy duchesses, marchionesses, countesses, viscountesses and baronesses," the Fairy Queen has the choice of slaughtering the whole company or changing her policy.) Among the male characters is the Arcadian shepherd, Strephon, who goes "by Nature's Acts of Parliament," and pays no heed to the male "blocking agent," the Lord Chancellor. He, like the Fairy Queen, binds himself by law, so much so, that he entraps himself in the complex legal issues:

> The feelings of a Lord Chancellor who is in love with a Ward of Court are not to be envied. What is his position? Can he give his own consent to his own marriage with his own Ward? Can he marry his own Ward without his own consent? And if he marries his own Ward without his own consent, can he commit

himself for contempt of his own Court? And if he commit himself for contempt of his own Court, can he appear by counsel before himself, to move for arrest of his own judgement?

Finally, the higher born but less worthy suitor (doubled here in the Lords Tolloller and Montararat, who are "both rich," "both earls," and "both plain") contends with the hero for the affections of the heroine. Gilbert's fairy extravaganza, then, is peopled with recognizable dramatic types.

The action, too, follows well-worn paths. Through Strephon, we follow the difficulties a young man encounters as he tries to rise in the world. A fairy "down to the waist," Strephon cannot find an occupation to suit his peculiar talents:

My body can creep through a keyhole, but what's the good of that when my legs are left kicking behind? I can make myself invisible down to the waist, but that's of no use when my legs remain exposed to view! My brain is a fairy brain, but from the waist downwards I'm a gibbering idiot. My upper half is immortal, but my lower half grows older every day, and some day or other must die of old age. What's to become of my upper half when I've buried my lower half I really don't know!

On the suggestion that he use his fairy brain in Parliament:

I'm afraid I should do no good there—you see, down to the waist, I'm a Tory of the most determined description, but my legs are a couple of confounded Radicals, and, on a division, they'd be sure to take me into the wrong lobby. You see, they're two to one, which is a strong working majority.

In the course of the play, however, he does enter Parliament, where he becomes "a Parliamentary Pickford—he carries everything!" This meteoric rise culminates in his final apotheosis as a full fairy, and his flight to Fairyland with his bride, Phyllis (along with the entire House of Peers, who, being obsolete because unintelligent, are transformed into fairies). As he pursues success in the sphere of business, Strephon encounters the usual difficulties in love, almost losing his beloved, Phyllis, when she misinterprets his kissing of "a maid of seventeen"—his fairy mother, Iolanthe. Like countless heroes of domestic drama, Strephon finally convinces Phyllis that she has wronged him, and she vows to do so no more: "Whenever I see you kissing a very young lady, I shall know it's an elderly relative." STREPHON: "You will? Then, Phyllis, I think we shall be very happy!" Other typical action—

the redemption of the fallen woman, the defeat of the other suitor, and the conversion of the blocking agents to a religion of feeling—has already been touched upon. And, of course, the play ends with multiple marriages, in true mid-Victorian style.

As critics have always recognized, Gilbert follows bourgeois Victorian dramatic rules of characterization, plot, and emotion to create—outrageous farce. The minute he dressed his female blocking agent as a Valkyrie and placed her opposite the Lord Chancellor of England to fight over Arcadian shepherds, Gilbert completely inverted, perverted, and finally subverted the aims of mid-Victorian drama. He does more than make the characters engagingly absurd. He exposes them. In *Iolanthe,* Gilbert shows the real figures and the true motives beneath the surface of middle-class drama and life.

Let us look first, as Gilbert usually does, at marriage. As we saw in the quotation from *Blue Beard,* early Victorians admitted that mercantile considerations sweetened most marriages. In the fifties, sixties, and seventies, however, the language of sentiment tried to disguise the importance of money to marriage—not, however, to deny money's intrinsic worth, but rather to make its value moral as well as practical. Now the quest for *earned* income proves the character of the hero. In the words of *Caste*'s honorable second lead, Sam Gerridge, the hero may hope to "merit a continuance of those favours which it [is] ever . . . 'is constant study to deserve." One of the favors such a hero deserves is a wife, a woman who makes the hearth her shrine and sets the moral standards of the family and the age.

There is no denying, however, what comedy has consistently shown— that the heroine must also be a social climber. She does not rise by effort but by marriage. Even the great heroine of *Caste* herself, Esther, marries D'Alroy and becomes at the play's end a rich aristocrat.

Iolanthe is unusual in Gilbert's canon for the relative mildness with which he explores the marriages that money sanctifies. Indeed, since everyone goes at the end to Fairyland where it may be that money is unnecessary (I would not, myself, be absolutely sure of this), everyone may marry whom she/he chooses. Still—we must note that the fairies all become "duchesses, marchionesses, countesses, viscountesses, and baronesses." Social climbing is not wholly mercantile—old-fashioned snobbery has its place as well. The only time money plays an important part in marital considerations is when Phyllis, thinking Strephon has deceived her, betroths herself to the Lords Tolloller and Montararat. In a ballad rich in the Gilbertian language of sentiment which reveals as it conceals the way in which a sentimental heroine pursues self-interest while appearing selflessly virtuous, Phyllis mourns:

> For riches and rank I do not long—
> Their pleasures are false and vain;
> I gave up the love of a lordly throng
> For the love of a simple swain.
> But now that simple swain's untrue,
> With sorrowful heart I turn to you—
> A heart that's aching,
> Quaking, breaking,
> As sorrowful hearts are wont to do!
>
> The riches and rank that you befall
> Are the only baits you use,
> So the richest and rankiest of you all
> My sorrowful heart shall choose.
> As none are so noble—none so rich
> As this couple of lords, I'll find a niche
> In my heart that's aching,
> Quaking, breaking,
> For one of you two—and I don't care which!

Here she plays the betrayed and broken-hearted lover who will bury her grief in selfless marriage to another, a suitor who is estimable but not beloved. At the same time, she plays the simple country lass who sees through aristocratic pretensions—"The riches and rank that you befall / Are the only baits you use." But, like many a sentimental heroine, the end result of Phyllis's nobility will be marriage to a rich peer (or, in Phyllis's case, *two* rich peers—one of Gilbert's favorite comic techniques is to force more than one character to fill the same role, *viz.,* Giuseppe and Marco in *The Gondoliers*).

Surely one of the finest examples in the canon of Gilbertian self-interest masquerading as self-sacrifice comes with the argument of Tolloller and Montararat as to who shall give up Phyllis:

> PHYL: There's really nothing to choose between you. If one of
> you would forgo his title, and distribute his estates
> among his Irish tenantry, why, then, I should then see a
> reason for accepting the other.
> LORD MOUNT: Tolloller, are you prepared to make this
> sacrifice?

LORD TOLL: No!

LORD MOUNT: Not even to oblige a lady?

LORD TOLL: No! not even to oblige a lady.

LORD MOUNT: Then, the only question is, which of us shall give way to the other? Perhaps, on the whole, she would be happier with me. I don't know. I may be wrong.

LORD TOLL: No. I don't know that you are. I really believe she would. But the awkward part of the thing is that if you rob me of the girl of my heart, we must fight, and one of us must die. It's a family tradition that I have sworn to respect. It's a painful position, for I have a very strong regard for you, George.

LORD MOUNT (*much affected*): My dear Thomas!

LORD TOLL: You are very dear to me, George. We were boys together—at least *I* was. If I were to survive you, my existence would be hopelessly embittered.

LORD MOUNT: Then, my dear Thomas, you must not do it. I say it again and again—if it will have this effect upon you, you must not do it. No, no. If one of us is to destroy the other, let it be me!

LORD TOLL: No, no!

LORD MOUNT: Ah, yes!—by our boyish friendship I implore you!

LORD TOLL (*much moved*): Well, well, be it so. But, no—no!—I cannot consent to an act which would crush you with unavailing remorse.

LORD MOUNT: But it would not do so. I should be very sad at first—oh, who would not be?—but it would wear off. I like you *very much*—but not, perhaps, as much as you like me.

LORD TOLL: George, you're a noble fellow, but that tell-tale tear betrays you. No, George; you are very fond of me, and I cannot consent to give you a week's uneasiness on my account.

LORD MOUNT: But, dear Thomas, it would not last a week! Remember, you lead the House of Lords! On your demise I shall take your place! Oh, Thomas, it would not last a day!

Noteworthy here is not just the way Gilbert reveals the ruthless self-interest beneath the sentimental language, but the way in which he shows Tolloller and Montararat *using* sentimental language deliberately to achieve selfish ends. Gilbert is not saying merely that Victorians are hypocritical self-deceivers, glossing over their less worthy motives to give priority to the virtuous ones; he condemns them rather from their own mouths as consciously manipulative self-servers, who use the language of virtue solely to achieve vicious ends. At the end of this bravura performance, Gilbert achieves transcendence when the two lords decide that Phyllis is not *worth* fighting over ("The sacred ties of Friendship are paramount") and leave, "lovingly," together.

Gilbert's satiric technique here exemplifies his method throughout the play. Gilbert's characters continually condemn themselves, simply by being themselves, and saying who they are. "This is what it is to have two capacities! Let us be thankful that we are persons of no capacity whatever," exclaims Lord Tolloller devoutly. "Two years," asks Strephon of Phyllis. "Have you ever looked in the glass?" "No, never," she replies. "Here, look at that (*showing her a pocket mirror*), and tell me if you think it rational to expect me to wait two years [to be married]?" Looking at herself, she exclaims in distress: "No. You're quite right—it's asking too much. One must be reasonable." This constant self-exposure, a self-indictment in Gilbert, will become in *Earnest* the beautiful expression of the Individual.

Iolanthe is a satire on both a literature and a class: a dramatic *Rape of the Lock*. Why, then, was it so popular with those it exposed (the same public that had denounced the earlier *Engaged* as heartless and vulgar, in large part because of its social-climbing, self-serving heroes and heroines) and why has its author been so frequently and so consistently misunderstood and accused of triviality ever since?

Since Gilbert's work first appeared, there has been remarkable critical consensus as to how he achieves his comic effects. From William Archer, writing in 1882, through to the present day and the excellent studies of such scholars as Jane W. Stedman, James Ellis, and Max Keith Sutton, critics have noted Gilbert's debt to, and subversion of, mid-Victorian drama. They have discussed his (mis)use of stock figures of melodrama and domestic drama, his invasion of fairyland, and, most importantly, that utterly serious treatment of an absurd subject, or the equally absurd treatment of a serious one, which, since his day, can only be named "Gilbertian." For all their agreement over the way Gilbert achieves his effects, however, critics cannot agree over the effects themselves. "Is Gilbert a satirist?" remains the crucial debate among them. Such eminent scholars as Edith Hamilton have answered "Yes," calling Gilbert "a mid-Victorian Aristophanes," while equally prominent critics like Archer have argued to the contrary. Among recent critics, Ellis claims that Gilbert takes the sting out of the satire, divorcing it from reality. To Ellis, Gilbert is a sublime humorist. Sutton, on the other hand, and Stedman both find Gilbert's humor and aims satirical. Stedman defends Gilbert on the oft-repeated charge that he propounds no positive reforms by likening his satire to that of Voltaire, a comparison G. K. Chesterton also proposed. John Bush Jones takes something of a middle ground in his introduction to a collection of Gilbert criticism by calling Gilbert a "satirist, or, at the very least, an ironist." Why, with such fundamental agreement over his manner, does Gilbert spark such unresolvable debate over his matter?

The answer, I think, lies largely in the very outrageousness of the performance, which is so overtly and exuberantly satiric that it loses some of its cutting edge in the sheer joy of piling up absurdities. While the great Swiftean satire is agonizingly comic, it is, after all, not very jolly. Critics like Shaw, whose mode is basically didactic, tend to see this quality as a trivialization of the subject. Consider Shaw's objections to *The Pirates of Penzance*:

> [Gilbert] could always see beneath the surface of things; and if he could only have seen through them, he might have made his mark as a serious dramatist instead of having, as a satirist, to depend for the piquancy of his ridicule on the general assumption of the validity of the very things he ridiculed. The theme of The Pirates of Penzance is essentially the same as that of Ibsen's Wild Duck; but we all understood that the joke of the pirate being "the slave of duty" lay in the utter absurdity and topsyturviness of such a proposition, whereas when we read The Wild Duck we see that the exhibition of the same sort of slave there as a mischievous fool is no joke at all.
>
> (*Music in London 1890–94*)

For Shaw, the notion that a man could feel morally bound to serve the pirates to whom he was apprenticed, as well as the "most ingenious paradox" of Frederic's having been born on Leap Day invalidate by their absurdity Frederic's dilemma and trivialize the satire on duty. He could not see, or perhaps could not acknowledge, that Gilbert *emphasized* by this absurdity the arbitrary nature of the social laws that govern us and the duties they impose. As Sutton points out, Gilbert "makes a comic, not a 'grimly serious' attack on compulsive moral idealism" (*W. S. Gilbert*).

In *Iolanthe*, for example, consider Strephon's complaint quoted above that being half a fairy is the curse of his existence ("My body can creep through a keyhole"). Certainly the details are ridiculous. Gilbert has, in

characteristic manner, logically followed out the consequences of an impossible premise. But beneath Strephon's practical problem of what to do
with his upper half when he's buried his lower half lies a very real awareness
of aging and death. Strephon's alliance with Phyllis, like Iolanthe's with
the Lord Chancellor or the Fairy Queen's with the plebeian Private Willis,
broaches the potent (and taboo) sexual and social issue of miscegenation
(not to mention that of incest latent in the pairing of Iolanthe and Strephon
or the Lord Chancellor and his son's fiancée!). Gilbert's instincts, in fact,
are anarchic, but his reason (or perhaps his unreason) demands the fierce
restraints of absurdity just because it recognizes its own passion. (LORD
CHANCELLOR: "I am here in two capacities, and they clash, my Lord, they
clash!") Strong sexual tension and grim awareness of the savage transito-
riness of life supply the energy in Gilbert's comedy by demanding equal
exuberance for their casting out.

Finally, to show that where the playwrights who most threatened him
were concerned Shaw never did get anything right (worth bearing in mind
for the discussion of *Earnest* immediately following), let us look at the
challenge he hurled at Gilbert:

> I defy any dramatist to set the fantastic and the conventional,
> the philosophic and the sentimental, jostling one another for
> stage-room without spoiling his play.
> (Review of *The Mountebanks, Music in London 1890–94*)

As we have seen in this discussion of *Iolanthe,* it was just this jostling which
comprised Gilbert's unique comic genius. (Indeed, it was just this jostling
which Shaw himself was to use to such good effect in plays like *Man
and Superman* and *Back to Methuselah.* Martin Meisel's superb *Shaw and
the Nineteenth-Century Theatre* details G. B. S.'s unacknowledged debts to
Gilbert.)

(I should like briefly to add that critics have wisely given Sullivan a
large share of the credit for the success of the Savoy operas over that of
plays like *Engaged.* Sullivan's superbly solemn music provides further "jostling" of genres, highlighting the absurdity of the language by its very
solemnity, as Ellis notes. Further, the choruses of fairies and peers, by their
dutiful repetition of every ridiculous phrase, add to the delight. Strephon
may not be able to prove that "Chorused Nature" bade him take his love,
but a chorus of fairy aunts certainly did. The music, as well, may explain
why Gilbert's passionately ambivalent struggle with bourgeois values is
not always immediately perceived. Somehow satire isn't as painful when
it is sung. And Sullivan, in this opera, produced some of his loveliest effects:

the Wagnerian fairy music at the opening, the Bach-like fugue which accompanies the Lord Chancellor, and his patented lyric ballads.)

Joe Orton, once dubbed by the *Observer* "the Oscar Wilde of Welfare State gentility," (im)pertinently observed:

> The writer can only chronicle the doings of fools or their victims. And because the world is a cruel and heartless place, he will be accused of not taking his subject seriously. . . . But laughter is a serious business, and comedy a weapon more dangerous than tragedy. Which is why tyrants treat it with caution. The actual material of tragedy is equally viable in comedy—unless you happen to be writing in English, when the question of taste occurs. The English are the most tasteless nation on earth, which is why they set such store by it.

Gilbert knew that all too well.

At last now we can revel in *The Importance of Being Earnest,* exploring its theatrical and ideologically motive origins. We shall see quite clearly that although Wilde, like Gilbert, attacked the bourgeoisie and its professed manners and morals, he did so from a perspective entirely different from that of the self-restraining Gilbert. A foreigner, a sexual outcast, and a "socialist" in his own idiosyncratic definition of the term, Oscar Wilde liberated comedy from all restraints except the rigorous confinements of aesthetics. In *Earnest,* he creates a comedy that is as firmly entrenched in the future as *Iolanthe* is in the past.

Oscar Wilde wrote *The Importance of Being Earnest: A Trivial Comedy for Serious People* in 1895, having already achieved considerable dramatic success with his "society comedies": *Lady Windermere's Fan, A Woman of No Importance,* and *An Ideal Husband.* He had also earned considerable notoriety for his epigrams, his novel *The Picture of Dorian Gray* (1890), and his poses. Unlike Gilbert, who was born into the English middle class and tried every one of its professions in turn (the military, law, civil service), Wilde came to London from Dublin via Oxford and never really took up any profession except the self-described one of "Professor of Aesthetics." That the middle class, its manners and morals, was to be Wilde's target as well as Gilbert's is evident in Wilde's critical writing of the period: the four essays of *Intentions* (1891, published separately from 1885–90) and his great aesthetic manifesto "The Soul of Man under Socialism" (1891). But his attitude toward it differs as much from Gilbert's as does his personality.

When we think of Oscar Wilde, usually the first thing we think of is his epigrammatic wit. And Wilde's wit takes the form of paradox: the inversion of bourgeois *sententiae* by the replacement of a key word with its opposite. "I hear her hair has turned quite gold from grief," "Divorces are made in heaven," "The home seems to me to be the proper sphere for the man"—I could pluck dozens of like phrases from *The Importance of Being Earnest,* each relying on the same principle for its humor. Paradox has always been seen as revolutionary, in the political sense of the term. It wars with the values of the public—from the nineteenth century on, the middle class. So, when Gwendolen says that "in matters of grave importance, style, not sincerity, is the vital thing," she is puncturing the sentimental ideal of the simple, blunt man or the "artless" maiden, the strength of whose emotion can be gauged by the poverty of his or her language. At the same time, she is stating what to Wilde is a great truth—not on the desirability of insincerity, but on the necessity of aesthetics, of beauty. Sincerity without style, without a feeling for the beautiful, is ugly. It shows not depth of emotion but lack of taste, and taste, or discernment, distinguishes sentient man from the brute.

Gilbert, as we saw, also deals in paradox. But for Gilbert, paradox rarely takes the form of epigram. His is a paradox of situation not of sentiment. A man who is a fairy down to the waist, a man who needs his own consent to marry his own ward, a man who has been apprenticed until his twenty-first birth*day* who turns out to have been born on Leap Day—these are Gilbert's characters. All undergo situations which are comic inversions of middle-class dilemmas (or at least the dilemmas of middle-class drama). The seriousness with which they deal with these situations, applying typical bourgeois solutions to absurd problems, gives the plays their satiric force. Most of the great jokes in Gilbert's plays demand an audience's awareness of the plot. Strephon's complaint, or the Lord Chancellor's superb paean of victory (in which he explains the steps whereby he convinced himself that he was a suitable candidate for Phyllis's hand) are funny because of their logical treatment of an illogical situation. They cannot be tossed off in a drawing room. (Of course, Gilbert does sometimes use the more self-contained, language-oriented paradox. Two of the greatest songs in *Iolanthe,* "Spurn not the nobly born" and "When Britain really ruled the waves," rely for their humor on a disjunction between the sentimental/ patriotic sentiment demanded by the music and the opening phrases and the inversion of it in the song. Two things should be noted here, however. Firstly, these are songs and, therefore, already set apart from the play by virtue of being sung. Secondly, Gilbert does not mock here the notion of virtue or imperial greatness as such; rather he satirizes the bourgeois idea that the one is found only among the lower classes or that the other depends on the leadership of England's hereditary rulers.)

Wilde's wit, then, reveals itself in epigram. Indeed, the possibility of detaching many of the verbal paradoxes from the play without robbing them of their comic force shows another characteristic of Wilde's language which distinguishes it from Gilbert's. Never a man to waste a good line, Wilde repeated many of his best from work to work. So, in *The Picture of Dorian Gray,* written five years before *Earnest,* Lord Henry Wotton says of a woman: "When her third husband died, her hair turned quite gold from grief." Indeed, many of the epigrams of *Dorian Gray* find themselves in Wilde's plays. This self-referentiality has the effect of heightening the artificiality of *Earnest,* for it pulls us out of the play mentally even as it moves the play temporally. Wilde, by constantly referring to his own works, creates a space outside the play *or* its satiric referent—an aesthetic place defined only as the personality of Oscar Wilde. Although Gilbert also believed in recycling himself—the Bab ballads provide the situations for the Savoy operas—his plays remain firmly in the sphere of bourgeois art and ideals. Being reminded of "The Fairy Curate" does not change one's perception of *Iolanthe* as being reminded of *Dorian Gray* changes one's view of *Earnest.* The Bab ballad is merely a source. The novel is a completely different work, one which forces a reappraisal of the play.

We have seen that the action of *Iolanthe* relies on its subversion of middle-class drama—it *is* the action of middle-class drama, carried through with utter seriousness from an absurd premise. The action of *The Importance of Being Earnest* also recalls middle-class drama. The worthy but impoverished suitor (Jack is deficient in parents, Algernon in funds), the aristocratic matriarch who plays the role of blocking agent, the rise of the young man to a position of worldly eminence—all these appear in Wilde's play, as they did in *Iolanthe.* Tirthankar Bose, in a brief but informative study of *Earnest's* structure, outlines these archetypal and stereotypical elements of the plot.

Earnest, however, despite these devices, moves differently from *Iolanthe.* Whereas in Gilbert's play the comedy depends in large part on the action—the longer the joke is spun out, the more closely it parallels its source, the more amusing it grows—in *Earnest* the various comic characters and actions *seem* to be dropped in carelessly, to achieve a localized comic/satiric effect. For example, Lady Bracknell never undergoes a change of heart which convinces her to grant Gwendolen to an obviously worthy Jack. Rather, Jack undergoes a change of identity, becoming a wealthy Ernest. Similarly, Gwendolen and Cecily seem at first to be the paired heroines of mid-Victorian drama: Gwendolen the idealist ("We live, as I hope you know, Mr. Worthing, in an age of ideals. . . . My ideal has always been to love someone of the name of Ernest"), Cecily the pragmatist

("But I don't like German. It isn't at all a becoming language. I know perfectly well that I look quite plain after my German lesson"). But they are not clearly enough delineated into these categories to function as strong satires on the two types—each woman is too completely herself (and too completely Wilde) to be a mere satire on a stereotype. What, then, is happening in *Earnest?*

The title of the play states Wilde's case from the outset. The whole action of the play, such as it is, is directed to the moment when Jack, who is really Ernest, will recognize "the vital Importance of Being Earnest." Since Jack is, indeed, Ernest, many critics have rightly pointed out that the play could as properly be called "The Importance of Being." *Earnest* concerns the self-realization of the individual, the development of the soul. Each character in the play is an aesthete, an artist of the personality, who devotes him or herself wholly to—him or herself.

Although the world of the play purports to be the social world of contemporary (1895) London, in fact it is wholly self-contained, beautifully artificial—a place where dandies will learn to be Individuals. As the play opens, certain characters show more awareness of the individual's purpose in life than do others. Algernon, perhaps, comes closest to exemplifying an artist of life: "He has nothing, but he looks everything. What more can one desire?" His goal throughout the play is the creation and the contemplation of the beautiful, the maintenance of perfect form, whether in expressive if inaccurate piano-playing, or buttonholes, or the eating of muffins ("One should always eat muffins quite calmly"), or marriage to Cecily. His reward for his self-absorption is Cecily, who freely admits that she is, as Algernon calls her, "in every way the visible personification of absolute perfection." Cecily, already a beautifully developed personality (I shall follow Ian Gregor in referring to the aesthetic characters in the play as "dandies," although, as I shall show below, I think Jack must develop *into* a dandy), "will not meddle with others," but "will help all," simply by being what she is. (I quote here from Wilde's essay "The Soul of Man under Socialism," to which I shall presently return.)

> ALGERNON: I want you to reform me. You might make that
> your mission if you don't mind, Cousin Cecily.
> CECILY: I'm afraid I've no time, this afternoon.
> ALGERNON: Well, would you mind my reforming myself this
> afternoon?
> CECILY: It is rather Quixotic of you. But I think you should
> try.

A self-created beautiful object of contemplation, Cecily aesthetically completes the developing Algernon. Their marriage will be a static union of beautiful surfaces.

Gwendolen, Algernon's cousin, like him seeks to develop herself. She rejects the notion that she is perfect: "Oh! I hope I am not that. It would leave no room for developments, and I intend to develop in many directions." More of an idealist and more of an artist than Cecily, Gwendolen must "love someone of the name of Ernest." She retains that ideal in the teeth of parental opposition: "But although [Lady Bracknell] may prevent us from becoming man and wife, and I may marry someone else, and marry often, nothing that she can possibly do can alter my eternal devotion to you." Her understanding of the aims of the individual make her the appropriate mate for Jack, who does not understand the importance of being Ernest. The true hero of the play, as Joseph Loewenstein points out, Jack learns the lesson *Earnest* teaches.

As the play opens, we see that Jack does not have the same strong sense of self that Algernon does. His opening lines sound a good deal like Algernon's, but, as Loewenstein notes, are quickly punctured:

> ALGERNON: Where have you been since last Thursday?
> JACK (*sitting down on the sofa*): In the country.
> ALGERNON: What on earth do you do there?
> JACK (*pulling off his gloves*): When one is in town one amuses
>   oneself. When one is in the country one amuses other
>   people. It is excessively boring.
> ALGERNON: And who are the people you amuse?
> JACK (*airily*): Oh, neighbours, neighbours.
> ALGERNON: Got nice neighbours in your part of Shropshire?
> JACK: Perfectly horrid! Never speak to one of them.
> ALGERNON: How immensely you must amuse them!

Although Jack speaks airily, tossing off Algernonian epigrams, he has not Algernon's aesthetic armor. He does not yet know who he is, so cannot develop his own personality. We see Jack's inferiority to Algernon in the way in which Algernon always gets the last cucumber sandwich, or Jack's own muffins, or an entire pint bottle of Perrier-Jouet, brut, '89, which Jack was reserving especially for himself. Until Jack realizes who he is, he cannot compete with a true dandy like Algernon, or marry one, like Gwendolen. It is noteworthy that when Jack turns out to be Ernest, when he discovers that he has been telling the truth his whole life, he becomes at the same time Algernon's *elder* brother, the heir to whatever estate there is, and presumably the man with first crack at future cucumber sandwiches.

Even Lady Bracknell and Miss Prism have something of the dandy in them. "A monster, without being a myth, which is rather unfair," Lady Bracknell did not let lack of substance stop her from gaining her own end: "When I married Lord Bracknell I had no fortune of any kind. But I never dreamed for a moment of allowing that to stand in my way." She is, however, obsessed with material possessions and must play the role of blocking agent, albeit with some unusual features. Miss Prism, the repressed governess, nonetheless gives full rein to her personality when she recovers her hand bag:

> Yes, here is the injury it received through the upsetting of a Gower Street omnibus in younger and happier days. Here is the stain on the lining caused by the explosion of a temperance beverage, an incident that occurred at Leamington. And here, on the lock, are my initials. I had forgotten that in an extravagant mood I had them placed there. The bag is undoubtedly mine. I am delighted to have it so unexpectedly restored to me. It has been a great inconvenience being without it all these years.

Only Canon Chasuble, with his recyclable sermons intended wholly for public consumption, seems outside the world of the dandy. But he, too, joins in the common inversion of middle-class pieties which characterize the dandies. Consider his reaction to Jack's brother Ernest's death:

> CHASUBLE: Was the cause of death mentioned?
> JACK: A severe chill, it seems.
> MISS PRISM: As a man sows, so shall he reap.
> CHASUBLE (*raising his hand*): Charity, dear Miss Prism,
>   charity! None of us are perfect. I myself am peculiarly
>   susceptible to draughts.

The characterization of Chasuble comes closer to Gilbertian satire than Wildean individualism, but fits Chasuble for the earnest Miss Prism.

Wilde's dandies, his artists of the soul, are not, then, mere parodies of bourgeois stereotypes. Searchers for an aesthetic wholeness, they conjure up comparisons with the middle class by being so resolutely detached from it. In fact, the characters in *Earnest* are "socialists," in Wilde's idiosyncratic definition of the term, and the world of the play is the world of Wildean "socialism." In "The Soul of Man under Socialism," Wilde put forth his views for an aesthetic utopia.

"The Soul of Man under Socialism," despite its title, is only nominally political in the sense that it posits any viable, or even coherent, system of government. Wilde's attempts to define the socialist "State" come no closer than "*The State is to make what is useful.*" (All italics are Wilde's.) However, "the State is not to govern," nor is it to interfere in any way in people's lives. It is not to demand the labor which will provide what is useful; rather,

> all unintellectual labour, all monotonous, dull labour, all labour that deals with dreadful things, and involves unpleasant conditions, must be done by machinery. Machinery must work for us in coal mines, and do all sanitary services, and be the stoker of steamers, and clean the streets, and run messages on wet days, and do anything that is tedious or distressing.

How a State will achieve this without governing, who will run the machines, who will ensure food and shelter—these are not explained. In fact, Wilde's "political" manifesto really sets forth his aesthetic creed: a creed of Individualism.

The power of "The Soul of Man under Socialism," and its connection to *The Importance of Being Earnest,* lies in its vision of the development of the individual, which parallels the development of the artist: "*Art is the most intense mode of individualism that the world has known.*" In the essay, Wilde defines the purpose of life as the realization of one's own personality. "The message of Christ to man was simply 'Be thyself.' " Man must treat his life as a work of art, concentrating solely on his own development:

> It has been pointed out that one of the results of the extraordinary tyranny of authority is that words are absolutely distorted from their proper and simple meaning, and are used to express the obverse of their right signification. What is true about Art is true about Life. . . . A man is called selfish if he lives in the manner that seems to him most suitable for the full realisation of his own personality; if, in fact, the primary aim of his life is self-development. But this is the way in which everyone should live. *Selfishness is not living as one wishes to live, it is asking others to live as one wishes to live. . . .* It is not selfish to think for oneself. A man who does not think for himself does not think at all. It is grossly selfish to require of one's neighbour that he should think in the same way, and hold the same opinions. Why should he? If he can think, he will probably think differently. If he cannot think, it is monstrous to require thought of any kind

from him. . . . Under Individualism people will be quite natural and absolutely unselfish, and will know the meanings of the words, and realise them in their free, beautiful lives.

The artist, as well, will be the person who realizes his personality in his art, without reference to the past or the present: "The past is what man should not have been. The present is what man ought not to be. The future is what artists are." *"A true artist takes no notice whatever of the public."* The result of this self-concern will be the creation of beauty in the development of the soul:

> It will be a marvellous thing—the true personality of man— when we see it. It will grow naturally and simply, flower-like, or as a tree grows. It will not be at discord. It will never argue or dispute. It will not prove things. It will know everything. And yet it will not busy itself about knowledge. It will have wisdom. Its value will not be measured by material things. It will have nothing. And yet it will have everything, and whatever one takes from it, it will still have, so rich will it be. It will not be always meddling with others, or asking them to be like itself. It will love them because they will be different. And yet while it will not meddle with others it will help all, as a beautiful thing helps us, by being what it is. The personality of man will be very wonderful. It will be as wonderful as the personality of a child.

The public, and its representative press, are accused throughout the essay of restricting the artist and the man through their desire to dominate, to authorize, and to control. Clearly, although he calls for social and economic equality, Wilde is advocating in "The Soul of Man under Socialism" a new elite, an aristocracy of artists and aesthetes. He pretends that it is available to all men, but lines like, "If he cannot think, it is monstrous to require thought of any kind from him," show that his new aristocracy will simply be drawn up along different lines from those of the old. That elite, and Wilde's elitism, dominate *The Importance of Being Earnest.*

The world of the play is the world of the elite, and, thus, of the dandy. Whereas in Wilde's social comedies dandies have to contend with middle-class society (whatever the ostensible class of the characters in the society plays, their attitudes are invincibly bourgeois), here middle-class society has been resolutely excluded, in what Regenia Gagnier, in her excellent study of Wilde and the Victorian public, calls "the representation of a Society in which all wishes come true." Nominally a portrait of contemporary London, the world of *Earnest* is rather a "socialist" State, in which every material possession is provided by some benevolent Power. In this world, everyone has the same great goal—Be thyself—within which his or her separate individual goals contend. The action of the play, therefore, for all the characters' physical movement, remains curiously static—quite different from the satiric exuberance of *Iolanthe*. "Being" implies internal rather than external development. The danger of a whole society of dandies, as Gagnier points out, is that it "renders insincerity static, a mere tool of personal power in service of the status quo" (as opposed to a single wit who, "subverting sincerity[,] can be liberating and dialectical"). I agree with Gagnier that the danger Wilde faces in *Earnest* is stasis, sterility even. But I disagree with her charge that "Wit, in this case, is entirely subservient to a traditional plot of marriage and money exchange." We must look at the plot, then, the physical action of the play, to see what is happening in *Earnest*'s world.

In his excellent brief study of *The Importance of Being Earnest,* Loewenstein points out that Wilde did not bother to develop a plot at all. Rather, he simply stole the most famous plot in Western literature—that of *Oedipus the King*—and adapted it to his play:

> That [Wilde] chooses what must be called the master-plot of Western drama is both characteristically sophomoric and characteristically self-aware: if one is uncomfortable with plotting, why not sabotage the model of plotting, so that plotting itself will look like a game not worth playing?

An archetypal plot to Loewenstein, a stereotypical plot to Gagnier; each, I think, persuades. The "plot" of *Earnest* does not represent the action of the play. Where does it lie?

I think the important action of the play is its play with antithesis—its obsession with balance and paradox. If we examine *The Importance of Being Earnest* closely, we will see that there is not a line that does not suggest its opposite, or find its complement elsewhere in the play. Each scene, each character, balances another, creating a continuously self-referential, self-reflexive entity. The play plays with ideas of exclusiveness, as it finally excludes all referents from itself, its world, or its author.

We have seen Wilde's sense of paradox at work in his epigrams. By changing the key word of a middle-class moral tag, Wilde turns the phrase and the sentiment in upon itself, forcing it to reveal an opposite meaning. But the paradox of paradox, of course, is that it relies on our awareness of what is being inverted for its effect. And if we are equally aware of what is said and its opposite, then each half of the equation retains its value. Meaning derives from a fusion of the two and is contained within their fused linguistic spheres. In Gilbert, this paradox works with particular appropriateness, for, as we have seen, Gilbert himself was a paradox: a Victorian bourgeois who saw through the bourgeois mask, but who, as passionately as he disbelieved in the mask, believed in its necessity. He summed up his dilemma succinctly in an early Bab ballad, "The Pantomime 'Super' to His Mask.'' In Wilde, whose paradoxes are contained in sentences rather than situations, the effect of the epigram is to close off meaning, to contain it within the linguistic frame. Camille Paglia brilliantly addresses this issue in her discussion of Wilde's language:

> The Wildean epigram, like a Giambologna bronze, is immediately identifiable by a slim spareness, an imperious separateness, and a perverse elegance. Speech in Wilde is made as hard and glittering as possible; it follows the Wildean personality into the visual realm. . . . Wilde's bon mots are so condensed that they become *things,* artifacts.

Beautifully balanced, symmetrically pure, Wilde's sentences prove that "in matters of grave importance, style, not sincerity, is the vital thing."

The antithetical nature of the play reveals itself as well in the play's structure. Wilde does not, as we have seen, satirize middle-class drama in any consistent way, nor does he create, as he did in *Lady Windermere's Fan,* an English *pièce bien faite,* nor does he come up with an original plot. *Earnest* contains, nonetheless, a tightly controlled, organized, and balanced structure. For each act, each action, each character, and each line finds a complement to close it off.

Let us start with the broad outlines of the action. (I will be using throughout the three-act version of the play. Controversy as to whether Wilde's changes were artistically as well as pragmatically motivated—cf. E. H. Mikhail, who calls the four-act version a "draft"—interests theatrical historians but need not, I think, alter our perception of the play. Wilde conflated the second and third acts into the second act, and deleted a biographically motivated scene about debts. The balancing of which I wish to speak remains in both versions. Wilde presented the three-act play as his and that version is known and read today.) The play opens indoors, in Algernon's flat, then the action moves outside to a garden, finally ending indoors again, this time in Jack's country estate. The town flat of the self-aware dandy, Algernon, becomes the country estate of the dandy who learns to know himself. These residences balance the "pastoral" garden in which no one seems to know him or herself. (Although Cecily and Gwendolen are the characters most sure of themselves, nonetheless, while in the garden, they each experience the dislocation of both being and not being engaged to Ernest.) At the beginning of the play, Jack comes to London to play Ernest, after which Algernon goes to Hertfordshire to play Ernest at the same time that Jack goes to Hertfordshire to kill Ernest; Jack turns out to *be* Ernest in Hertfordshire. As Ernest comes to life, Bunbury dies.

In addition to parallel movement between acts, there are scenes within acts which balance each other. In the first act, Jack proposes to Gwendolen and has his suit denied by Lady Bracknell; in the second act Algernon proposes to Cecily and has his suit denied by Jack (a rebuff which he ignores), after which Gwendolen and Cecily reject Jack and Algernon; in the third act, Gwendolen and Cecily re-engage themselves to Jack and Algernon, with Lady Bracknell both denying permission for an engagement and seeking it; at last both couples become engaged—as do Miss Prism and Canon Chasuble.

In addition to the engaged couples, other pairs form throughout the play—frequently in opposition. Algernon and Lane open the play as master and servant—aristocrat and working-class man who will be balanced in act 3 by Lady Bracknell and her erstwhile servant Miss Prism. Algernon and Jack confront each other both as the serious and shallow Bunburyist and as lovers in pursuit: Algernon of a woman he has never met, Jack of Gwendolen. Gwendolen and her mother Lady Bracknell arrive as the sentimental heroine and her practical mother, or youth and age. In the second act, Miss Prism and Cecily are "Egeria and her pupil," although Miss Prism cannot teach and Cecily will not learn (and Miss Prism's name is Laetitia). The bulk of the second act concerns the majestic formation and re-formation of the couples of Algernon and Cecily (lovers), Algernon and Jack (false brothers), Cecily and Gwendolen (friends), Cecily and Gwendolen (enemies), Gwendolen and Jack (lovers), Cecily and Algernon (lovers), Cecily and Gwendolen (companions in grief), and finally Jack and Algernon (companions in the baptistry). The third act repeats and reworks these combinations and permutations, ending with Jack and Algernon as true brothers.

Perhaps we may more clearly apprehend the extent to which Wilde balances each element of the play if we compare two short scenes. Since this play purports to deal with the courtship ritual, I shall compare Jack's proposal to Gwendolen in act 1 with Algernon's proposal to Cecily in act 2.

The two scenes balance each other in antithetical ways: they follow opposite actions to similar ends (the engagement of the couple) at the same time repeating lines and ideas. In addition, each scene maintains its own balance, its own wholeness of conception within the larger frame of the act. Gwendolen eschews small talk (about the weather), urging Jack to state his business since "Mamma has a way of coming back suddenly into a room that I have often had to speak to her about." After her famous speech on ideals—hers has been to love someone named Ernest—Gwendolen asks Jack why he has not yet proposed: "I often wish that in public, at any rate, you had been more demonstrative." Jack urges her to consider the beauty of the name "Jack," but when this proves fruitless, resolves to be christened at once. He then discovers that they are not yet engaged—he has not properly proposed. Despite the fact that Gwendolen is "fully determined" to accept him she demands that he fall on his knees. In this position, they are in fact interrupted by Lady Bracknell: Gwendolen and Jack consider themselves engaged, however, even though they may never be allowed to marry.

Cecily and Algernon, meanwhile, have just met, and may be about to part—the opening of the scene is punctuated by Merriman's frequent arrivals announcing the dog cart to take Algernon to the station, for a departure which Algernon and Cecily continually postpone. As Cecily points out: "The absence of old friends one can endure with equanimity. But even a momentary separation from any one to whom one has just been introduced is almost unbearable." As Algernon compliments Cecily, preparatory to proposing, Cecily starts writing his words down in her diary. She then informs him that they have been engaged for three months: "Worn out by your entire ignorance of my existence, I determined to end the matter one way or the other, and after a long struggle with myself I accepted you"; the seriousness of the betrothal was proven when it survived being temporarily broken off. Cecily had been entranced by his personality, that of the wicked younger brother, and feels secure in marrying someone of the name of Ernest, a name which "seems to inspire absolute confidence." Despite the fact that "half of the chaps who get into the Bankruptcy Court are called Algernon," Cecily will marry none but Ernest. Algernon leaves her hurriedly to attend to "a most important christening," and Cecily, upset that he should expect her to wait as long as half-an-hour, consoles herself by writing his proposal into her diary.

In each case, the female takes command of the situation—a reversal of traditional expectations—but in opposite ways. Each woman proclaims the value of the name Ernest in winning her affections, each man realizes the necessity of being christened without delay. Each woman begs her lover to make his private emotions public—Gwendolen wishes Jack had shown his feelings more in public and ends their courtship scene with praise for his appearance. His eyes, she says, "are quite, quite blue. I hope you will always look at me just like that, especially when there are other people present." Cecily writes Algernon's compliments into her diary: "It is simply a very young girl's record of her own thoughts and impressions, and consequently meant for publication." She ends their idyll with a comment on his appearance: "I like his hair so much. I must enter his proposal in my diary." For each woman, style is more important than sincerity. Gwendolen equates how Jack looks with how he looks at her and how he is seen to look at her. Cecily, knowing that Algernon's hair curls "naturally," "with a little help from others," excuses him his bad life because he has such good taste: she has her record of his proposal (and the letters she sent herself from him) to prove it. Each woman equates style with substance, but in different forms; this determines the final disposition of their courtships. Gwendolen marries a man of the name Ernest, with which she fell in love, while Cecily fell in love with the wicked younger brother of Jack and marries him.

We can see in these scenes in brief what engages the entire play. No action, no prop, no line is wasted. Even such an innocuous line as "Charming day it has been, Miss Fairfax," resonates, first in Gwendolen's immediate dismissal of it ("Whenever people talk to me about the weather, I always feel quite certain that they mean something else"), and later in Cecily's account of her broken engagement:

> CECILY (*reading her diary*): "Today I broke off my engagement with Ernest. I feel it is better to do so. The weather still continues charming."
>
> ALGERNON: But why on earth did you break it off? What had I done? I had done nothing at all. Cecily, I am very much hurt indeed to hear you broke it off. Particularly when the weather was so charming.

Cecily's diary will be matched with Gwendolen's diary in an attempt to assign priority to Ernest's affections. (And Gwendolen's diary will remind us of Cecily's Political Economy: the diary provides "something sensational to read in the train," while the chapter on the Fall of the Rupee turns out to be "somewhat too sensational" for a girl like Cecily.)

Cecily's diary, "meant for publication," recalls Jack's "private cigarette case" which Algernon took the liberty of reading and which alerted him to Cecily's existence. Both cigarette case and diaries will be balanced by Miss Prism's three-volume novel "of more than usually revolting sentimentality" which replaced the baby in her handbag. Lionel Trilling was wrong here (as he was in calling Gilbert and Carroll nonsense writers) in considering the baby/handbag mix-up Gilbertian. In fact, by playing on the notion of novel as child and equating both with not only a diary but a cigarette case, Wilde is most uniquely Wildean here. We should now be able to draw our conclusions about what makes *The Importance of Being Earnest* so different, finally, from *Iolanthe*.

To balance every idea, every line, every character throughout the play is to cut the play off from all outside referents. And when words, or ideas, have no referents, we have no way of assigning them value. What is the difference between a baby, a three-volume novel, and a cigarette case? Is it important to be Ernest or to be earnest? When Wilde complains in "The Soul of Man under Socialism" that under the "tyranny of authority" "words are absolutely distorted from their proper and simple meaning, and are used to express the obverse of their right signification," he addresses the issue which *Earnest* embodies. For *Earnest* sets words free. Far from being a sharp satire on middle-class drama of life, *Earnest* makes of itself a discrete work of art, wholly self-contained, insistently self-reflexive. Phrases, attitudes, characters may seem to reach out to a world of bourgeois art and life, but before the play's end they are forced back into the universe of the drama. In "The Soul of Man under Socialism," Wilde points out that

> a picture and a statue are not at war with Time. . . . In one
> moment their unity may be apprehended. In the case of literature
> it is different. Time must be traversed before the unity of effect
> is realised. And so, in the drama, there may occur in the first
> act of the play something whose real artistic value may not be
> evident to the spectator till the third or fourth act is reached.

In time, everything in *Earnest* leads insistently back to—Oscar Wilde's *The Importance of Being Earnest*.

As we saw earlier, Wilde's repetition of epigrams from work to work (and to drawing room as well) creates an aesthetic space that can finally only be defined as the personality of Oscar Wilde. Each of the characters in *Earnest* turns out not to be fulfilling his or her own individuality, but expressing a facet of Wilde's. That is why the end, with the multiple marriages, cannot be seen as fruitful. Each couple may create a fusion of incomplete individuals, but together they make up only parts of another individual, just as *Earnest* becomes only part of the literary and social expression of a man. Wilde tries in "The Soul of Man under Socialism" to address the issue of sterility. Incessant individuality, he insists, will be socially oriented because "man is naturally social." Nature, indeed, will play her part in other ways as well: "To ask whether Individualism is practical is like asking whether Evolution is practical. *Evolution is the law of life, and there is no evolution except towards Individualism.*" How will we know if we have achieved a social individualism?

> Man has sought to live intensely, fully, perfectly. When he can do so without exercising restraint on others, or suffering it ever, and his activities are all pleasurable to him, he will be saner, healthier, more civilized, more himself. Pleasure is Nature's test, her sign of approval. When man is happy, he is in harmony with himself and his environment.

At the last, then, Wilde shirks the question. Nature will be the great socializer. (The end of *Earnest* plays with this idea when Jack "naturally" turns out to be Ernest.) Indeed, "The Soul of Man under Socialism" finally parallels *Earnest* by making itself as resolutely self-reflexive and self-referential as the play. The end of the essay leads only to the beginning; the aesthetic manifesto becomes the expression of Wilde's personality. While *Earnest* remains a great source of pleasure, then, it achieves its end by its disharmony with its environment, either literary or social. Perfect in itself, it must be perfect *by* itself, the literary essence, if you will, of a man who was never in harmony with his environment.

I think *Earnest*'s self-referentiality (in both senses) accounts for the recurrent critical difficulty in classifying *Earnest*. Often critics, after tossing off a few references to French drama or English bourgeoisie, conclude that the play does not fit into any dramatic category. It is *sui generis*. If they place it at all, it becomes the first English work in a new tradition—the exploration of nothingness, existential theater, theater of the absurd. The "Importance of Being (Earnest)," they argue (most notably David Parker), has as its corollary the importance of not being, of nothingness. This theory seems to me far more compelling than the one that would make of *Earnest* just rehashed Gilbert. *Iolanthe,* one of the supreme satires in English drama, operates from a firmly entrenched position behind enemy lines. *The Importance of Being Earnest,* on the other hand, by denying any reality outside of the play or its author, becomes an essay into the Absurd. It plays with dramatic tradition, but sublimely is not of it.

Chronology

1854	Oscar Wilde born in Dublin on October 16 to Protestant parents: William Wilde, a distinguished oculist, and Jane Elgee Wilde, a writer (under the pseudonym "Speranza").
1864–71	Wilde educated at Portora Royal School, Enniskillen.
1871–74	Studies Classics at Trinity College, Dublin, under John Pentland Mahaffy.
1874–78	Studies at Magdalen College, Oxford, where his professors include Walter Pater. Wins the Newdigate Prize for poetry and receives a B.A. in Greats (Classics) with First Class Honours.
1876	Death of father.
1879	Moves to London.
1881	Publishes *Poems*. Writes *Vera; or the Nihilists* (first produced in New York in 1883). Gilbert and Sullivan's *Patience* produced.
1881–82	Lectures in the United States and Canada on the Aesthetic movement.
1883	Writes *The Duchess of Padua* (first produced in New York under the title *Guido Ferranti* in 1891).
1884	Marries Constance Lloyd, a family friend from Dublin.
1885	Son Cyril born.
1886	Son Vyvyan born. Wilde meets Robert Ross.
1887–89	Editor of *Woman's World*.
1888	Publishes *The Happy Prince and Other Tales*.
1889	Publishes "The Portrait of Mr W. H." in *Blackwood's Magazine*.
1890	Publishes "The Picture of Dorian Gray" in *Lippincott's Magazine*.

1891	Publishes "The Soul of Man under Socialism" in *Fortnightly Magazine; Intentions* ("The Decay of Lying" [first published 1889], "Pen Pencil and Poison" [first published 1889], "The Critic as Artist" [first published 1890], and "The Truth of Masks" [first published 1885]); *The Picture of Dorian Gray* (book form); *Lord Arthur Savile's Crime and Other Stories;* and *A House of Pomegranates.* Writes *Salome* in Paris. Meets Lord Alfred Douglas.
1892	*Lady Windermere's Fan* produced. *Salome* banned by the Lord Chamberlain. Publishes limited edition of *Poems.*
1893	*A Woman of No Importance* produced; *Salome* published in French. *Lady Windermere's Fan* published.
1894	*Salome* published in English with illustrations by Aubrey Beardsley. *The Sphinx* and *A Woman of No Importance* published.
1895	*An Ideal Husband* and *The Importance of Being Earnest* produced. Wilde sues Douglas's father, the Marquess of Queensberry, who has objected to Wilde's relationship with his son, for libel; Queensberry acquitted. Wilde arrested the same day for sexual offences; after a first trial results in a hung jury, he is convicted at a second trial and sentenced to two years' hard labor.
1895–97	Imprisoned at Reading.
1896	Death of mother.
1897	Writes letter to Lord Alfred Douglas which will be published (in edited form) as *De Profundis* (finally published complete in 1962). On release from prison, Wilde travels to Continent under the name Sebastian Melmoth.
1898	Publishes *The Ballad of Reading Gaol.* Constance Wilde dies.
1899	Publishes *The Importance of Being Earnest* and *An Ideal Husband.*
1900	On November 30, Oscar Wilde dies in Paris, where he is buried.

Contributors

HAROLD BLOOM, Sterling Professor of the Humanities at Yale University, is the author of *The Anxiety of Influence, Poetry and Repression,* and many other volumes of literary criticism. His forthcoming study, Freud: Transference and Authority, attempts a full-scale reading of all of Freud's major writings. A MacArthur Prize Fellow, he is general editor of five series of literary criticism published by Chelsea House. During 1987–88, he served as Charles Eliot Norton Professor of Poetry at Harvard University.

IAN GREGOR is Professor of Modern English Literature at the University of Kent. He is the author of several books, and has edited a collection of critical essays on the Brontës.

ROBERT J. JORDAN is Professor and Head of the School of Drama at the University of New South Wales, Australia. He has coedited the plays of Thomas Sotherne and writes on Restoration comedy.

DAVID PARKER is Professor of English at the University of Malaya. He has published essays on Chaucer and Shakespeare.

RODNEY SHEWAN is the author of *Oscar Wilde: Art and Egotism.*

KATHARINE WORTH is Professor of Drama and Theatre Studies in the University of London at Royal Holloway College. She is the author of *The Irish Drama of Europe from Yeats to Beckett* and *Oscar Wilde,* and editor of *Beckett the Shape Changer.*

CAMILLE A. PAGLIA teaches literature at the Philadelphia College of Art. She is the author of the forthcoming *Sexual Personae: Art, Power, and Paganism in Western Culture.*

JOSEPH LOEWENSTEIN is Assistant Professor of English at Washington University. He is the author of *Responsive Readings: Versions of Echo in Pastoral, Epic, and the Jonsonian Masque.*

149

REGENIA GAGNIER is Assistant Professor of English at Stanford University and the author of *Idylls of the Marketplace: Oscar Wilde and the Victorian Public*.

SUSAN LAITY is Associate Editor at Chelsea House Publishers, New Haven, and a free-lance critic. She has published on John le Carré and W. S. Gilbert and the development of Victorian drama.

Bibliography

Barth, Adolf. "Oscar Wilde's 'Comic Refusal': A Reassessment of *The Importance of Being Earnest.*" *Archiv für das Studium der Neuren Sprachen und Literaturen* 216 (1979): 120–28.

Beckson, Karl, ed. *Oscar Wilde: The Critical Heritage.* London: Routledge & Kegan Paul, 1970.

Bentley, Eric. *The Playwright as Thinker: A Study of Drama in Modern Times.* New York: Harcourt Brace Jovanovich, 1967.

Bird, Alan. *The Plays of Oscar Wilde.* London: Vision, 1977.

Bloom, Harold, ed. *Modern Critical Views: Oscar Wilde.* New York: Chelsea House, 1985.

Bose, Tirthankar. "Oscar Wilde's Game of Being Earnest." *Modern Drama* 21 (1978): 81–86.

Chamberlin, J. E. "Oscar Wilde and the Importance of Doing Nothing." *The Hudson Review* 25 (1972): 194–218.

Cohen, Philip K. *The Moral Vision of Oscar Wilde.* Cranbury, N.J.: Associated University Presses, 1978.

Dickson, Sarah Augusta, ed. The Importance of Being Earnest: A Trivial Comedy for Serious People *in Four Acts as Originally Written by Oscar Wilde.* 2 vols. Arents Tobacco Collection Publication 6. New York: New York Public Library, 1956.

Donohue, Joseph W., Jr. "The First Production of *The Importance of Being Earnest:* A Proposal for a Reconstructive Study." In *Essays on Nineteenth Century British Theatre,* edited by Kenneth Richards and Peter Thomson, 125–43. London: Methuen, 1971.

Ellmann, Richard. *Eminent Domain: Yeats among Wilde, Joyce, Pound, Eliot, and Auden.* New York: Vintage, 1970.

———. "Introduction: The Critic as Artist as Wilde." In *The Artist as Critic: Critical Writings of Oscar Wilde,* edited by Richard Ellmann. Chicago: University of Chicago Press, 1969.

———, ed. *Oscar Wilde: A Collection of Critical Essays.* Englewood Cliffs, N.J.: Prentice-Hall, 1969.

Fineman, Joel. "The Significance of Literature: *The Importance of Being Earnest.*" *October* 15 (1980): 79–90.

Fletcher, Ian, and John Stokes. "Oscar Wilde: Plays." In *Anglo-Irish Literature: A*

Review of Research, edited by Richard J. Finneran, 96–108. New York: Modern Language Association of America, 1976.

Foster, Richard. "Wilde as Parodist: A Second Look at *The Importance of Being Earnest.*" *College English* 18 (1956): 18–23.

Freedman, Morris. *The Moral Impulse: Modern Drama from Ibsen to the Present.* Carbondale: Southern Illinois University Press, 1967.

Fussell, B. H. "The Masks of Oscar Wilde." *The Sewanee Review* 80 (1972): 124–39.

Ganz, Arthur. *Realms of the Self: Variations on a Theme in Modern Drama.* New York: New York University Press, 1980.

———. "The Meaning of *The Importance of Being Earnest.*" *Modern Drama* 6 (1963–64): 42–52.

Gide, André. *Oscar Wilde: In Memorium.* Translated by Bernard Frechtman. New York: Philosophical Library, 1949.

Green, William. "Oscar Wilde and the Bunburys." *Modern Drama* 21 (1978): 67–79.

Hardwick, Michael. *The Osprey Guide to Oscar Wilde.* Reading, England: Osprey, 1973.

Harris, Alan. "Oscar Wilde as Playwright: A Centenary Review." *Adelphi* 30, no. 3 (1954): 212–40.

Hart-Davis, Rupert, ed. *More Letters of Oscar Wilde.* New York: Vanguard, 1985.

———, ed. *Selected Letters of Oscar Wilde.* Oxford: Oxford University Press, 1979.

Holland, Vyvyan. *Oscar Wilde and His World.* New York: Scribner's, 1978.

———. *Son of Oscar Wilde.* 1954. Reprint. Westport, Conn.: Greenwood, 1973.

Hyde, H. Montgomery. *Oscar Wilde: A Biography.* New York: Harcourt Brace Jovanovich, 1975.

Knight, G. Wilson. *The Golden Labyrinth: A Study of British Drama.* London: Phoenix House, 1962.

Laver, James. *Oscar Wilde.* London: Longmans, 1968.

Lavrin, Janko. *Aspects of Modernism from Wilde to Pirandello.* London: Stanley Nott, 1935.

Matlock, Kate. "The Plays of Oscar Wilde." *The Journal of Irish Literature* 4, no. 2 (1975): 95–106.

Mikhail, E. H. *Oscar Wilde: An Annotated Bibliography of Criticism.* London: Macmillan, 1978.

———. "The Four-Act Version of *The Importance of Being Earnest.*" *Modern Drama* 11 (1968): 263–66.

———, ed. *Oscar Wilde: Interviews and Recollections.* 2 vols. New York: Harper & Row, 1979.

Nassaar, Christopher S. *Into the Demon Universe: A Literary Exploration of Oscar Wilde.* New Haven: Yale University Press, 1974.

Nethercot, Arthur H. "Prunes and Miss Prism." *Modern Drama* 6 (1963–64): 112–16.

Omasreiter, Ria. *Oscar Wilde.* Heidelberg: Winter, 1978.

Partridge, E. B. "The Importance of Not Being Earnest." *Bucknell Review* 9, no. 2 (1960): 143–58.

Pearson, Hesketh. *The Life of Oscar Wilde.* 1946. Reprint. London: Methuen, 1954.

Pine, Richard. *Oscar Wilde.* Dublin: Gill & Macmillan, 1983.

Poague, L. A. "*The Importance of Being Earnest:* The Texture of Wilde's Irony." *Modern Drama* 16 (1973): 251–57.

Powell, Kerry. "Wilde and Ibsen." *English Literature in Transition 1880–1920* 28 (1985): 224–42.

Reinert, Otto. "The Courtship Dance in *The Importance of Being Earnest.*" *Modern Drama* 1 (1959–60): 256–57.

———"Satiric Strategy in *The Importance of Being Earnest.*" *College English* 18 (1956): 14–18.

Roditi, Edouard, *Oscar Wilde*. New York: New Directions, 1947.

Roitinger, Anita. *Oscar Wilde's Life as Reflected in His Correspondence and His Autobiography*. Salzburg: Institut für Anglistik und Amerikanistik, University of Salzburg, 1980.

Rowell, George. *The Victorian Theatre: A Survey*. Oxford: Oxford University Press, 1956.

San Juan, Epifanio, Jr. *The Art of Oscar Wilde*. Princeton: Princeton University Press, 1967.

Shewan, Rodney. *Oscar Wilde: Art and Egotism*. London: Macmillan, 1977.

Small, Ian. "Semiotics and Oscar Wilde's Accounts of Art." *British Journal of Aesthetics* 25 (1985): 50–56.

Spininger, Dennis J. "Profiles and Principles: The Sense of the Absurd in *The Importance of Being Earnest.*" *Papers on Language & Literature* 12 (1976): 49–72.

Stone, Geoffrey, "Serious Bunburyism: The Logic of *The Importance of Being Earnest.*" *Essays in Criticism* 26 (1976): 28–41.

Sullivan, Kevin. *Oscar Wilde*. Columbia Essays on Modern Writers 64. New York: Columbia University Press, 1972.

Taylor, John Russell. *The Rise and Fall of the Well-Made Play*. London: Methuen, 1967.

Toliver, Harold E. "Wilde and the Importance of 'Sincere and Studied Triviality.' " *Modern Drama* 5 (1962–63): 389–99.

Ware, James M. "Algernon's Appetite: Oscar Wilde's Hero as Restoration Dandy." *English Literature in Transition 1880–1920* 13 (1970): 17–26.

Acknowledgments

"Comedy and Oscar Wilde" by Ian Gregor from *The Sewanee Review* 74, no. 2 (April-June 1966), © 1966 by the University of the South. Reprinted by permission of the editor.

"Satire and Fantasy in Wilde's *The Importance of Being Earnest*" by Robert J. Jordan from *Ariel* 1, no. 3 (July 1970), © 1970 by A. Norman Jeffares and the University of Calgary. Reprinted by permission.

"Oscar Wilde's Great Farce: *The Importance of Being Earnest*" by David Parker from *Modern Language Quarterly* 35, no. 2 (June 1974), © 1974 by the University of Washington. Reprinted by permission.

"The Providential Pun" (originally entitled "The Comedy of Manners: The Dandy's Progress") by Rodney Shewan from *Oscar Wilde: Art and Egotism* by Rodney Shewan, © 1977 by Rodney Shewan. Reprinted by permission of Macmillan, London and Basingstoke.

"The Triumph of the Pleasure Principle" (originally entitled *"The Importance of Being Earnest"*)by Katharine Worth from *Oscar Wilde* by Katharine Worth, © 1983 by Katharine Worth. Reprinted by permission of the Grove Press and Macmillan, London and Basingstoke.

"Oscar Wilde and the English Epicene" by Camille A. Paglia from *Raritan: A Quarterly Review* 4, no. 3 (Winter 1985), © 1985 by *Raritan: A Quarterly Review*. Reprinted by permission.

"Wilde and the Evasion of Principle" by Joseph Loewenstein from *The South Atlantic Quarterly* 84, no. 4 (Autumn 1985), © 1985 by Duke University Press. Reprinted by permission.

"Idyll of the Marketplace" (originally entitled "Comedy and Consumers") by Regenia Gagnier from *Idylls of the Marketplace: Oscar Wilde and the Victorian Public* by Regenia Gagnier, © 1986 by the Board of Trustees of the Leland Stanford

Junior University. Reprinted by permission of the publishers, Stanford University Press.

"The Soul of Man under Victoria: *Iolanthe, The Importance of Being Earnest,* and Bourgeois Drama" by Susan Laity, © 1987 by Susan Laity. Published for the first time in this volume. Printed by permission.

Index